024978

D0477411

University College for the Creative Arts

25 JUN 1991

13 MAY 1993   − 6 NOV 2003

20 APR 1994   1 9 APR 2004

09. DEC   1 0 JAN 2007

4 FEB 1999

2 2 MAR 2001

− 6 DEC 2001

WEST SURREY COLLEGE OF ART AND DESIGN

24978

Please return this book by the latest date shown

Contents

A HISTORY OF THE UMBRELLA

A History of the Umbrella

T. S. Crawford

DAVID & CHARLES : NEWTON ABBOT

7153 4799 3

COPYRIGHT NOTICE

© T. S. CRAWFORD 1970

All rights reserved. No part of this publication may be reproduced, stored in a retrieval system, or transmitted, in any form or by any means, electronic, mechanical, photocopying, recording or otherwise, without the prior permission of David & Charles (Publishers) Limited

WEST SURREY COLLEGE
OF ART & DESIGN
GUILDFORD CENTRE LIBRARY

Set in eleven point Imprint two points leaded
and printed in Great Britain
by Latimer Trend & Company Limited Plymouth
for David & Charles (Publishers) Limited
South Devon House   Newton Abbot   Devon

391.
44
CRA

24978

Illustrations

7

' "Where is my toadstool?" loud he lamented,
And that's how umbrellas were first invented.'

—OLIVER HERFORD,
The Elf and the Dormouse

Foreword

W HAT A CURIOUS subject to write about! Such was the reaction of many people on hearing that I was compiling a history of the umbrella. Obviously, they could not have appreciated either the extent or depth of the subject, and imagined, no doubt, that my book was to be merely a detailed account of fashion. Whereas, in fact, fashion is but the visible tip of this particular iceberg, and there is much more to this work than details of umbrella and parasol styles.

Psychologists would doubtless trace my interest in 'brolliology' to an event in my youth. Whilst on an introductory visit to the public school I was later to join, my parents noticed that most of the pupils seemed to prefer an umbrella to a raincoat for protection against the weather. Some months later I returned to the school as the rawest of new boys, armed with a brand-new brolly, only to learn that I had committed something of a solecism, an umbrella being the exclusive privilege of the sixth form and secretaries of societies. As I attained neither station, and was forced to rely upon a duffle-coat for my entire stay at the school, this is perhaps a study born of thwarted aspirations.

But I did not become fascinated by the umbrella until I read some comments which David Piper made in 1952, and discovered that no really comprehensive book about it had yet been written in English:

> Brolliology, the science of the umbrella, awaits development. It owns no Nuffield professorship, no Rockefeller research studentship; it exists, if at all, still nebulous, in one of the loftier intellectual atmospheres, into which even the aspiration of post-graduate scholarship in search of a thesis has yet to penetrate.[1]

Yet many writers have contributed information on some
aspect or other of the subject, and several have remarked that it
merits expansion. William Bates thought that 'The history of
this indispensable utensil would surely form an interesting
volume, and afford a fine scope for the display of archaeological
and anecdotical lore.' And how right he was in prophesying that
'No little labour and research would be required in tracing the
origin, uses and mechanical development of the instrument from
the earliest times'.[2] Octave Uzanne attempted such a task and
discovered that:

> An archaeologist might amuse himself with writing a special work on
> the role of the sunshade in Greece; documents would not fail him; nay,
> the book would soon grow big, and might bristle with notes from all
> quarters, abounding in the margins, after the example of those good
> solid volumes of the sixteenth century, which none but a hermit would
> have the leisure to read conscientiously today.[3]

Though Uzanne exaggerated the potential size of such a work,
a study of old Greek vases depicting the parasol might be re-
warding to an enthusiast, if to nobody else. Uzanne's own book
is a delightful one, not least because of its imaginative illustrations of nude women bearing parasols in ancient times. Though
first published as long ago as 1883 in France, and concentrating
mainly on that country, it is nonetheless still well worth reading.
Its author confesses that his is only 'a general and summary
sketch', and he does, in fact, overlook the umbrella's significance
in the Catholic Church, a subject exhaustively treated by
Charles de Linas in the following year.[4]

But for the follower of fashion the book is adequate enough,
even though Uzanne admits that had he attempted to record all
the many transformations of the sunshade between 1830 and
1870 he would have had 'to write a volume quite full of coloured
vignettes [to give] a feeble idea of the history which fashion
creates in an object of coquetry'. (Another Frenchman, René-
Marie Cazal, enthused when he considered 'how many volumes
would be required to describe in its thousand fantasies the
kaleidoscope of feminine thought in the use of the parasol.[5])
When Uzanne had completed his researches into the history of
the umbrella he found:

We have gathered so ample a harvest of notes, our sheaf has become so large, so very large, that it was impossible for us to bind our arms about it, after having co-ordinated its various parts. It is but a poor few strays, then, which lie stranded here . . . sole vestiges of a project which became Homeric as it grew great in the workshop of the imagination.[6]

Though I wish I could have seen all those superfluous notes, now lost to posterity, I fancy they referred mainly to the swiftly changing styles of the nineteenth century. Today, the value of an account devoted exclusively to the multitude of fashions in umbrellas, as was envisaged by Cazal and Uzanne, would be open to question, for sufficient idea of the varying designs, fabrics and colours may be gleaned from general costume books. There is, however, a need for a comprehensive work on the umbrella, and though one, concentrating on Europe, was published in Italy in 1956,[7] there has been no such book written in English and telling of the brolly's development in this country. It is hoped that the present work will go some way towards meeting this deficiency, in giving some idea of the origins of the umbrella, its importance in ceremonial regalia, in religious art and architecture, and its contribution to social history, as well as describing its place in fashion.

I should make one explanation concerning my use of the words 'umbrella' and 'parasol'. It had been my intention to keep strictly to their modern significances, for the former, though originating from the Latin *umbra*, meaning 'shade', now infers protection against rain, whilst 'parasol' denotes a sunshade. However, for centuries people have bandied the two words around, and my necessary reliance on timeworn and ambiguous references has made such discrimination impossible. But the reader will notice some differentiation throughout and especially in the account of the umbrella and parasol since 1750.

In the course of my researches for this book I have been pleasantly surprised at the interest which others have shown in the subject. The response to my many inquiries has been re-markably enthusiastic—with the sole exception of certain branches of the umbrella industry who were, understandably, more concerned with present-day production problems than nostalgic memories of the past. Specific mention of those to whom I am particularly indebted for assistance will be found in the Acknowledgments on page 201.

Finally, just as this work was completed, the first man landed on the moon and among the equipment he used for transmitting television pictures back to Earth was an object which unquestionably owed its design and shape to the umbrella and was actually called, at least unofficially, an 'umbrella-antenna'. A fitting conclusion, it seemed, to my researches, the most striking feature of which had been the discovery of the widespread and diverse influence of the umbrella-motif, now extended beyond the frontiers of space to a world other than our own.

Page 17 (*above*) King Ashurbanipal of Assyria under his chariot-parasol, *circa* 1350 BC; (*below*) a curious Greek umbrella held by Silenus; a scene from a Bacchanalia, *circa* 440 BC (from a vase in the Berlin Museum)

Page 18 (*left*) Woman with parasol, from a Sicilian mosaic of the fourth century AD; (*right*) Roman toilet articles—bag and sunshade

I *The Origins of the Umbrella*

THE SAFEST STATEMENT of fact that can be made about the first umbrella is that it was constructed over 3,000 years ago, for its origins are so obscure that we do not even know whether its invention was prompted by the need to keep off the sun or rain. All we can be certain of is that from early times religious and mythological symbolisms have been closely associated with the umbrella's development and importance. Detailed investigation into its evolution is avoided by most writers, who content themselves with stating that prototypes were used in Egypt and Assyria, where they constituted a privilege accorded only to royalty.

Most probably, Egypt was the country in which the umbrella originated and where it first became an item of religious and ceremonial regalia, rather than an article of fashion. By 1200 BC, models of smart and intricate design were being held over the most distinguished nobles, to denote their higher plane of royalty overshadowing the under-world of lower planes, and especially to symbolise the vault of heaven over a king.

At first, these appear to be grandiose attributes of what eventually became a commonplace article, but an examination of contemporary legends and beliefs suggests some explanations. The Egyptians believed the sky was formed by the body of their celestial goddess Nut, who spanned the earth, touching it only with her toes and finger-tips. Shu, the Egyptian equivalent to Atlas, supported Nut with one hand on her breast, the other on her mid-thigh, so that her star-spangled belly formed the arch of the heavens. The two are sometimes thus represented on the inner lids of sarcophagi, in a position that can be likened to a gigantic umbrella, Nut's body forming the cover and Shu acting as the stick and supports.

So the earliest umbrella could have been constructed to represent this concept of the heavens; to be carried over the king to show his heavenly status rather than to protect him from the sun. A startling comparison, perhaps, yet to this day many peoples the world over regard the sky as a dome or canopy, or even an umbrella, above which live warriors like those on earth. The Jains of India, whose cult began to flourish five centuries before Christ, believe the universe to be in the shape of a colossal human form, topped by a massive place of perfection in the shape of an umbrella of luminous white gold. This is the ultimate heaven, called the *isat-pragbhara*, or Slightly Tilted Umbrella, to which souls ascend after they have attained perfection. The followers of Buddha have a similar belief, frequently featured in the architecture of their burial monuments, which are surmounted by umbrella-type finials.

In time, the Egyptians came to look upon the umbrella as representing the stability and durability of the royal person entitled to its use, and could have borrowed these attributes from the *djed* or *tet*, a kind of pillar with four capitals or discs, which was connected with the harvest, and had evolved from the trunk

The Egyptian *djed*, which possessed some similarities to later architectural expressions of the umbrella-motif

of a fir. The *djed* was the special emblem of Osiris, son to the goddess Nut, and one of the most appealing and important of Egyptian deities. He was originally a nature god embodying the spirit of vegetation which died at the harvest and was reborn when the grain sprouted anew. Later, he was worshipped throughout the country as the god of the dead.

Osiris is said to have succeeded to the Egyptian throne and to have done much to civilise his country by abolishing undesirable customs such as cannibalism, and by teaching his people how to use grain and grapes for nourishment in the form of bread and wine. Eventually he was able to appoint a regent and embark on the peaceful conquest of Asia, which he accomplished mainly through music and education. Osiris's kingly qualities were expressed in the *djed* in the same way as the characteristics expected of his mortal successors were symbolised by the umbrella. Furthermore, the Egyptians believed the *djed* was the soul of Osiris and so used it to denote the core of life; often they represented it as a cosmic pillar holding up the sky and so ensuring the space between heaven and earth in which the king's authority might be recognised. As such, it was often fitted into the arches of windows, not out of architectural necessity but to give the impression of support. It will be seen in the next chapter that the cosmic pillar and core of life form part of the umbrella motif in Asian funeral monuments which, furthermore, have multistoreys vaguely similar to the four discs of the *djed*.

Osiris has another indirect link with the umbrella for, as representative deity of the vine, corn and tree, he later became identified with the Greek god Bacchus (also called Dionysus) whose followers carried sunshades in their processions. There are several connections between the Osiris cult and later uses of the umbrella concept, though the link is by no means proven. One can only pinpoint what may be mere coincidences and observe that the umbrella retained many of the characteristics first noted in Egypt as its use spread across Asia and along the Mediterranean coasts.

In time, great importance came to be attached to the shade cast by the royal umbrella, and it was likened to the protection afforded by the king's power. In the first chapter of the apocryphal book of Baruch, ascribed to the first century BC, there occurs the passage: 'We shall live under the shadow of Nebuchodonosor, King of Babylon, and under the shadow of Balthasar, his son'; and though the umbrella is nowhere mentioned in the Bible, Nebuchodonosor would almost certainly have included it as part of his regalia. In ancient Egyptian texts a hieroglyph in the shape

of an umbrella ⌐⊤ sometimes denoted sovereignty. More im-

portant, it also signified the *khabit* or *khaibit*, the shadow of a person in which, it was thought, resided his generative powers. Thus the *khaibit* was considered one of the body's most important attributes, for, after death, resurrection of the spiritual body was not complete until the physical form possessed a shadow. The carrying of the early umbrella could, therefore, have had some sexual significance, and indeed the reproductive concept of shadow and umbrella can be traced throughout Asia, to West Africa, and to Western Europe. (The French verb *ombrager* and the German *beschatten*, both deriving from words meaning 'shadow', were once used to refer to the covering of the cow by the bull. Significant, too, are the number of countries where the heads of bride and/or bridegroom are covered by umbrellas or canopies of cloth, the latter a custom once practised in England.)[1]

The umbrella proper, used to both shade and honour a sovereign, is depicted on Egyptian sculptures of the eleventh century BC, and a model made of palm leaves, with the pointed ends of the leaves facing upwards, is featured on a Theban relief of an Ethiopian princess. A papyrus of this same period also mentions a royal umbrella in a context that has prompted A. T. Olmstead to describe the reference as 'the first recorded joke of history'.[2] About 1114 BC, Pharaoh sent a certain Wenamon to Zakar Baal, the anti-Egyptian Prince of Gebal, to procure cedar for a new royal ship. During one of their rather strained conversations, with Wenamon becoming increasingly doubtful of his ability to fulfil his master's orders, the shadow of Zakar Baal's umbrella fell upon the Egyptian envoy, whereupon a member of the prince's entourage jokingly remarked: 'The shadow of Pharaoh, your lord, falls upon you.' The joke was not a particularly good one, nor was it exactly respectful to Zakar Baal, since it suggested his power, as represented by the umbrella, was inferior to Pharaoh's, and he suitably reprimanded the jester.

Whatever form Zakar Baal's umbrella took it would certainly have been heavy and cumbersome, which no doubt explains why its bearer was unable to hold it still over his prince. Even so, it was probably a considerable improvement on the previous custom of using shields to shade the sovereign. A sculpture found at Beni-Hassan shows a royal leader being carried in a palanquin; behind him walks an attendant with his arm almost fully upraised and holding a man-sized shield above the noble's head, which must be fully 9 ft above the ground.

From Egypt, the use of the umbrella spread to Assyria, where again it was originally the king's privilege to have it carried over his head, usually during ceremonial processions. George Rawlinson has noted that:

> The officers in close attendance upon the monarch varied according to his employment. In war he was accompanied by his charioteer, his shield-bearer . . . and sometimes by his parasol-bearer. In peace the parasol-bearer is always represented as in attendance, except in hunting expeditions, or where he is replaced by a fan-bearer. The parasol, which exactly resembled that still in use throughout the East, was reserved exclusively for the monarch. It had a tall and thick pole, which the bearer grasped with both his hands, and in the early times a somewhat small circular top. Under the later kings, the size of the head was considerably enlarged, and at the same time, a curtain or flap was attached, which, falling from the edge of the parasol, more effectually protected the monarch from the sun's rays. The head of the parasol was fringed and tasseled, and the upper extremity of the pole commonly terminated in a flower or other ornament. In the later time both the head and the curtain which depended from it were richly patterned. If we may trust the remains of colour upon the Khorsabad sculptures, the tints preferred were red and white, which alternated in bands upon the parasol as upon the royal tiara.[3]

Rawlinson states that a fan-bearer replaced the parasol-bearer on hunting expeditions, though a parasol is featured in a hunting scene at Taq-i-Bustau, near Kermanshah, 240 miles from Nineveh. A fresco of the fifth century after Christ shows the king leaving for a stag-hunt with a parasol-bearer running behind his horse; a later scene shows the king riding at full gallop, and naturally neither bearer nor parasol are to be seen. As carrying

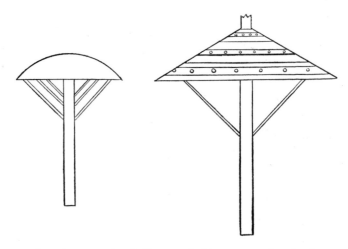

Assyrian parasols: (*left*) as carried by an attendant in the seventh century BC, and (*right*) as mounted on a chariot, of earlier date

the umbrella was a job that needed both hands, one wonders how the bearer fared when the sun was beating down on his sovereign's back, and his own, for the curtain would be interposed between him and his master, so blocking his own view. No one seems to have spared much thought for the parasol-bearer, though Rawlinson does have a few words to say about him:

> The parasol-bearer was attired as the bow and quiver-bearers, except that he was wholly unarmed . . . Though not a military officer, he accompanied the monarch in his expedition, since, in the midst of war, there might be occasions of state when his presence would be convenient.[4]

It has never been clear whether this job of bearer was considered menial or honourable. Certainly it could not have been a pleasant task to hold an elaborate parasol over one's sovereign, be it in the heat of the sun or the heat of battle. (Though when the king was using his chariot, he was sheltered by the larger umbrella fitted to the vehicle.) On the other hand, the bearer might enjoy some of the king's limelight and occasionally make use of his shade, perhaps even boasting of the sexual significance of the umbrella (if he were not one of the many eunuchs who were employed as servants). It is perhaps misleading to refer to the Assyrian bearers as officers (as did Rawlinson), for the word now suggests rank; they were probably men of low birth, or favoured slaves, who would regard their task, despite or because of its toughness, with some pride.

Some time before the eighth century the Greeks, no doubt recognising the sexual significance of the Egyptian *khaibit*, as represented by the shape of an umbrella, made symbolical use of actual sunshades in several associated sets of fertility rites, including those of Demeter and Persephone, who had strong associations with harvest prosperity. 'Of all the mystic rites of Demeter, which the Hellenes call Thesmophoria, I shall leave unspoken all except so much as piety permits me to tell. The daughters of Danaos were they who brought this rite out of Egypt and taught it to the women of the Pelasgians' wrote Herodotus.[5] (The Pelasgians were reputedly the earliest inhabitants of Greece.)

Persephone, daughter to Demeter, is represented on old vases as holding an umbrella; like Osiris, she symbolised the vegetation which died during the winter and was born again in the spring. Later her followers in the Thesmophoria prayed to Athena to prevent too great a summer heat, and during this supplication the priestess was protected by a huge white parasol. Various of her attendants were similarly covered, for in Aristophanes' play *Thesmophoriazusae*, of the fifth century BC, the chorus of women boast that they have not thrown away their parasols as their menfolk have their shields—an indication of the comparative value placed on the former.[6]

Similar to the Thesmophoria was the Skiraphoria, once known to some imaginative writers as the Feast of Boughs, or Umbrella Feast. Modern opinion is that the name indicates that something was carried, and it has long been assumed that the otherwise unidentified *oklpa* associated with the Feast were parasols, as a priest and priestess went from the Acropolis to a place called Skira under a large white umbrella.

A parasol was also carried over the priest at Alea in southern

Greece, where the Arcadians worshipped Liber, an old Italian deity concerned with productivity and the vine, in a ceremony to invoke the sun's favour on their agricultural labours. The Romans' version of these celebrations also laid emphasis on birth and fertility, and on the seed of plants and animals, so that their rites included worship of the phallus. About the sixth century BC, the Graeco-Roman god Bacchus absorbed the cult of Liber, and established connections with the other ceremonies mentioned above; for instance, his statue headed the procession in the Thesmophoria, and some of his followers carried umbrellas on these occasions. Bacchus possessed many of the attributes of Osiris, including those of death and resurrection (Plutarch made this and other comparisons in *Isis et Osiris*); thus in 130 AD, when the Emperor Hadrian tried to establish his young friend Antinous as a god after the boy's death, the Egyptians came to worship him as Osiris whilst other races preferred to regard him as Bacchus.

In some versions of the early Bacchanalia, women featured prominently and often exclusively in the celebrations, but when men were allowed to join in the proceedings became obscene, and eventually those males who were reluctant to participate ended up as sacrifices! Such debauchery took place in Rome at the beginning of the second century that in 186 BC the Senate issued a decree suppressing the cult; the Thebans also had to legislate against the ceremonies, but neither measure had complete success, so great were the numbers of the Bacchantes.

For several hundred years the umbrella served as a symbol of productivity at festivals in honour of Bacchus and must also have represented the sexual aggression of the celebrants themselves. But about the fifth century BC the umbrella became rather less of an erotic symbol in Greece, and was increasingly used as a means of providing shade. So in the great Bacchanalia held at Alexandria in the reign of Ptolemy Philadelphus (285–46 BC) the statues and fruit offerings were decorated with ivy and vine branches and protected by a purple and white canopy or umbrella. (It is not clear which, though the terms are often interchangeable, one with the other.)

A few umbrella-historians do perhaps overstress the use of the parasol in these old ceremonies, but all too often it is overlooked or dismissed by less partisan authorities who do not appreciate the importance of its symbolism in such scenes, in which, admittedly, it is often a bizarre object. Yet at one time it was so closely associated with festivals that Prometheus, in Aristophanes' *Aves*, first performed in 414 BC, covered himself with an umbrella, explaining that 'if Zeus should see me, he'll just think I'm taking part in a procession'.[7] (Prometheus had abandoned himself to a secret passion for Venus and wished to hide himself from Zeus, with whom he was never on good terms.)

Furthermore, whenever an umbrella does appear in Greek sculptures showing a male deity, it is nearly always in connection with the cult of Bacchus. In fact, when Paulus Paciaudus reproduced in his *De Umbellae Gestatione* the top part of an engraved stone showing three cherubs, one of whom bore an umbrella, he confidently restored the missing half with a representation of the god. Of the other two cherubs, one carried a further attribute of Bacchus, the thysus (a reed tipped with a pine); the other held a lyre, for the god of wine was frequently associated with music and many of his retinue delighted in its pleasures.

One of the many feasts contemporary with the Bacchanalia were the Panathenaic Games, held in Athens, during which daughters of the alien group of Metoeci (who were allowed to live in the city without any civil rights) had to carry parasols for the Athenian maidens as a form of humiliation. In this instance the shades were featured more for the convenience of the maidens than as a reverential symbol, for the Greeks also classed the parasol as a domestic utensil, Aristophanes mentioning it in conjunction with the loom, weaving-beam and basket.[8] But the menfolk seldom carried umbrellas for their own benefit, and Anacreon, *circa* 520 BC, mockingly referred to a certain Artamon using an ivory-framed parasol 'as do women'.[9] For many centuries the only occasion when a Greek man might excusably be seen holding an umbrella was over his female companion; nor would the male rulers normally have a ceremonial model held over them, hence the Athenian general Xenophon's reference to the Assyrians being dissatisfied with the shade given by trees and rocks and having 'people to stand by them to provide artificial shade'.[10]

Aristophanes had one of his characters, Agoracritus, say to Demos: 'Your ears opened like a parasol and then furled again' which suggests that some, at least, of the contemporary models could be opened and shut.[11] Indeed, the main problem would be to get the covering material to fold up satisfactorily when the umbrella was closed. Later models were certainly very similar to modern designs, with fabric spread over slender ribs, and stretchers attached to a ring that slid the length of the handle. Frames were light enough for the parasols to be carried by women in one hand.

Graeco-Italian artists featured the parasol on pottery showing mystic weddings or scenes of courtship. At a comparatively late date they also included it on funereal vases to indicate that the deceased woman was of high rank, sometimes showing it in scenes from her life, or else depicting it held over her corpse as it was being laid out for burial. In these cases it is probable that the umbrella also possessed some form of funeral symbolism. The early Greeks had planted trees on the graves of their dead to provide the all-important shade, and the umbrella may have become an occasional substitute for this.

A fashionable development of the third century BC was the sunshade hat, which was shaped very much like a parasol without the handle and was also effective against the rain. Such hats are still worn in Asia and are remarkably like the covers of opened parasols. (The word 'sombrero', one term for this type of head-gear, was once used to denote a sunshade, and some writers have suggested that one article derives from the other.) The women of Tanagra, twenty-five miles north of Athens, had their own unusual model of straw, painted red and white, and secured to the head by means of a cord. It had the advantage of being very light and did not have to be carried around like a parasol, but it could scarcely have set off the charms of the wearer.

About the third century BC the umbrella spread from Greece to Rome where, according to contemporary literature, it had no particular significance and was merely a useful fashion accessory for protection against the heat. Ovid referred to 'a golden parasol to ward off the keen sun' which Hercules had carried over Omphale, Queen of Lydia, whom he served as a slave for a time.[12] Martial mentioned the *umbracula* which was carried against the excessive heat of the sun and could also be used as a veil against the wind.[13] He also recommended that though one might begin a journey with a bright sky, a *scortea* should be taken in case of unexpected showers.[14] Strictly, *scortea* means an object made from leather, and though this suggests a cloak or hooded garment, some translators take the word in this context to mean an umbrella. Such a waterproof model would have had to be more robust and cumbersome than the more luxurious sunshade, which might have had a cover dyed purple, ornamented with gold and fitted with a handle of Indian ivory studded with gems.

Some women had their parasols dyed a certain colour to denote which chariot team they favoured in the amphitheatre. Such events are usually envisaged as taking place against a background of dust and heat, when protection from the sun would be desirable, but umbrellas were also taken along when rain threatened. Some spectators objected to having their view blocked by sunshades and sunhats, and there was much argument as to whether they should be allowed in the amphitheatre until the Emperor Domitan ruled in their favour.

Audiences at some of the larger arenas, like the Colosseum, were protected by a great awning, secured to outer masts and probably supported by others. On one occasion Caligula, irritated by the lack of public appreciation of the show he had put on, ordered the awning to be removed and kept the people in the scorching heat for several hours. No doubt sunshades were in great demand that day!

Like the Greeks, the Romans used the parasol in their courtship techniques, and Ovid, expounding on the art of love, recommended that every attention be paid the lady:

> Yourself hold up her parasol outspread,
> Yourself through crowds make clear her path ahead.[15]

Martial, when his friend Lygdus failed to keep an appointment, exclaimed in jealous annoyance: 'Lygdus, may you carry the parasol of a short-sighted old lady.'[16] Should a man carry an umbrella for his own benefit he was considered effeminate, and Juvenal, in recording the 'sorrows of a reprobate', spoke of:

> ... a pretty fellow, to have presents sent him of green sunshades or big amber balls on a birthday, or on the first day of showery spring, when he lolls full-length in a huge easy chair, counting over the secret gifts he has received upon the Matron's day.[17]

The umbrella featured on an interesting coin, or medal, believed to have been issued under Roman authority in Judaea when Herod Agrippa was monarch, AD 37–44. One side showed an umbrella, the other three ears of corn, which, it has been

Coin issued in Judaea *c* AD 40, showing a sunshade with obscure religious significance, but perhaps representing harvest fertility

suggested, marked the fertility of the Jewish provinces, or referred to the Feast of the Tabernacle, which has been compared with the Bacchanalia, both corn and umbrella being attributes of Bacchus.[18] It appears that the coin was identified by the seventeenth-century numismatist, Ezechiel Spanheim, whose findings have ever since gone unchallenged, despite his admission that he was hesitant about the significance of the symbols on the coin. Conceivably, then, the coin might have been more closely related to Bacchus than to the Jews and the Tabernacle, possibly being a token of the powerful society formed by followers of the god. The Tabernacle itself has been put forward as a forerunner of the canopy and umbrella, for it had 'a veil of blue and purple and scarlet . . . which shall divide unto you between the holy place and the most holy'.[19] Such terminology recalls one purpose of the religious umbrella, to shield a divine person from the greater divinity of the sun.

The notorious Roman emperor Heliogabalus (218–22) also favoured the use of the parasol, and it is portrayed on severa medallions of his reign. Whatever his reasons for adopting such an emblem, he must have noted the custom of carrying a parasol during his early life in Syria, and been aware of its regal significance. It was from Syria that he journeyed to Rome to claim the imperial title, and he might well have taken the royal umbrella with him as a symbol to support his own questionable position as emperor.

Some authorities have thought the parasol to be connected with sun worship, and suggest that Heliogabalus used it as an emblem of priesthood in his vaguely defined Syrian cult of the 'Unconquerable Sun God'. Furthermore, he had connections with the cult of Bacchus, believing it was that god who had set up two colossal phalli outside a temple in Syria. 'Since he combined youth, beauty, and fine dress, he made men think of a beautiful picture of the young Bacchus,' wrote Herodian.[20] Heliogabalus could have identified himself with the god and thus adopted the umbrella, though this explanation is not as likely as the others put forward.

The costume parasol persisted as a fashion in Rome for many centuries—and, indeed, its use is said to have been continuous up to the present day. In 399, Claudian referred to it in much the same way as had Ovid: 'a golden umbrella warding off the sun's keen rays', but added that it should be discarded in time of war, which seems to suggest that men, and soldierly ones at that, were then carrying sunshades.[21] Claudian also mentioned that slaves, apparently eager for self-improvement, would no longer carry parasols over the heads of maidens.[22]

However, it was then more common for the Romans to wear the *petasus*, a broad-brimmed hat similar to that favoured by the Greeks, and some women even arranged their hair to shade their faces. But in the sixth century a treatise of uncertain authorship, *De Disiplina Scholarium*, mentioned a youth, the son of a praetor, who died from jaundice caught in the heat of the dog-days because he had not taken his customary sunshade with him. By this time, it would seem, prudence had overcome the fear of being deemed effeminate, and the umbrella and parasol had become accepted as costume accessories, but not necessities, for both sexes.

In China it is possible that the umbrella evolved quite separately from its Egyptian counterpart, though there are theories that the custom of carrying a sunshade spread from the Orient westward to Europe and Africa, rather than in the opposite direction as here suggested. Certainly the oriental umbrella, like the Egyptian, stretches so far back into history that it is now impossible to determine which part of the world first saw the umbrella, and Egypt has been favoured in the present account mainly because of interesting points arising from its legends, and partly because we in the West have such a scanty knowledge of early China.

European writers have, however, recorded one relevant Chinese tale, dated prior to 1000 BC, concerning the wife of Lou-pan, who one day told her husband, who was a skilled carpenter: 'You make houses with extreme cleverness, but they can't move; the object I'm making for personal use can be carried any distance,'—and eventually she produced a parasol.

There are other traditions in China that the *San*, or 'shade against sun and rain', originated with standards and banners waved in the air. Silk models, known as the *Lo-san* and *Jih-chao*, were used in early processions, and the custom of parading hundreds of parasols as if they were flags was a popular practice in Imperial China. The ancient *Tcheou-Li*, or *Rites of Tcheou*, of the eleventh century BC, directed that the *dais*, identifiable from its description with a parasol, should be placed upon ceremonial chariots. The *Rites* describes its construction as being of a silk or feathered cover on twenty-eight arcs, or curved ribs. The supporting staff measured three-eighteenths of a Chinese foot (probably slightly longer than the English one) in circumference, with a lower section six-tenths of a foot round, so that the stick could be partially telescoped.

Oriental technology appears to have been well in advance of western designs, for collapsible umbrella stays have been recovered from the tomb of Wang-Kuang (dated *circa* 25 BC) at Korean Lo-Lang. At much the same time Wang-Mang's ceremonial four-wheeled carriage had a *hui-kai*, or parasol, which could be collapsed by means of a secret mechanism called *pi-chi*.[23]

Chinese art of the first century AD features a flat parasol, obviously honorific, which was held over dignitaries, and shows larger models fixed to the chariots of the gods of Thunder and Wind, in tribute to their divinity. Utility parasols seem to have been introduced about this time, and these were made of oiled paper and bamboo, materials which are still used today. At first, servants held these parasols over their masters, though it is believed that people began to carry their own in the fifth century.

2　The Umbrella in India and the East

FOR OVER 2,000 years the umbrella in India has been a symbol of reverence, and has maintained its prominent position in ceremonial to this day. The earliest models depicted in Indian bas-reliefs are very like those favoured by the Assyrians, and the Persian title, *Sattrapas*, was possibly corrupted to *Ch'hatra-pati*, or Lords of the Umbrella, a designation given to the Mahratta princes who reigned at Poonah and Sattara and held in higher esteem than even the title of rajah or maharajah.

Yet there is evidence of influences from further west than Persia. The prominent Indian deity, Varuna, carries an umbrella called *Abhoga*, reputedly made from the hood of a cobra and impervious to water (in contrast to the umbrellas connected with other deities, whose models appear to have been sunshades). Varuna is the personification of the sky, a fertility god and a bestower of rain, and as such is comparable with some of the deities mentioned in Chapter 1. He is also the Indian version of Mithras, the Persian sun-god, who may have been the deity worshipped by the Roman emperor Heliogabalus.

Varuna's umbrella was borrowed by the god Vishnu in his Fifth Incarnation, when he assumed the shape of a pigmy and descended into hell. In an attempt to compare Bacchus with Indian divinities, this legend has been likened to a scene entitled *Bacchus ad Inferos*, showing the Greek god as a boy on the dolphin sacred to him, bearing an umbrella and about to descend to the depths of the ocean.[1] In his Sixth Incarnation, Vishnu, in another of his forms, fought with Ravana, king of Ceylon, and was aided by aggressive apes bearing branches of palm-trees, a tale that is

Page 35 Herod and Herodias; an Italian example of the custom, common in
Asia and Africa, of indicating royalty by an umbrella (a thirteenth-century
scene in the Baptistry of Florence)

Page 36 (*left*) Model of a stupa showing four umbrellas, representative of the heavens, topping the dome; (*right*) Hindu marriage scene, with the bridal pair covered by a symbolic umbrella

readily identifiable with that concerning Bacchus's invasion of India, when he led an army of satyrs bearing vine boughs. Those seeking a mythical origin for the umbrella in India could do no better than suggest that the god himself introduced it during his visit.

Certainly there are many pertinent links between the mythology of India and that of other countries, but however closely one examines their relevant myths, legends and various deities, all that can be claimed with any assurance is that the umbrella appears to have been generally associated with those gods who were connected with fertility, often those of the harvest, and this association may well have stemmed from the umbrella's symbolism of the heavens, from which came the rain and sun so essential to good crops.

The Indians came to regard the umbrella as a more general symbol of respect several centuries before the birth of Christ, the followers of Buddha being particularly eager to honour their god with a white model. In many sculptures, a parasol held over an

A Buddha surmounted by three honorific umbrella canopies:
from the caves at Ellora in Hyderabad

C

apparently empty space signifies that Buddha is present though invisible—as in the reliefs representing the Great Departure at Amaravati, one of the main centres of early Buddhist art in Southern India. In some art images Buddha does not appear, but is represented instead by a religious symbol such as a wheel or throne, often overshadowed by a parasol. The umbrella itself is one of Buddha's Eight Treasures which feature in his footprints and are often used as talismans; even today a woman with an umbrella-shaped mark on her hand is thought to be assured of good fortune in life.

One of the numerous *Jataka* tales relates how the god Brahma held a white umbrella over Buddha's head when he was born in the sixth century before Christ. Other legends recount how on this occasion Buddha's mother, Queen Maya, was holding a branch of the sal tree as her son was painlessly delivered out of her right-hand side. Because of this the tree itself is protected by an umbrella in sculptures at the famous Sanchi stupa.

At a very early date Indian kings adopted the umbrella just as their western counterparts had done. They also had much the same symbolism in mind, as is shown in a passage in the fifth act of Kalidasa's *S'akuntala* (written between AD 350 and 600) when King Dushyanta talks of how:

> the cares of supporting the nation harass the sovereign, while he is cheered with a view of the people's welfare, as a huge umbrella, of which a man bears the staff in his own hand, fatigues while it shades him. The sovereign, like a branching tree, bears on his head the scorching sunbeams, while the broad shade allays the fever of those who seek shelter under him.

Accounts of royal funerals held centuries ago mention that the corpse was often adorned by a white sunshade and that 'at the sound of all the musical instruments, hundreds of men offered in honour of the extinguished shoot of Kourou a crowd of fly-flaps, white sunshades and splendid robes'.[2] Here also the royal custom followed a precedent attributable to Buddha, whose body is said to have been protected by canopies and umbrellas at its funeral procession at Kusinara, *circa* 487 BC.

The sunshades at such obsequies were to honour the deceased's sovereignty, but the umbrella also possessed an important funereal significance on such occasions. At Perwuttum, it is shown in sculptures depicting *lingas* (phallic symbols) and cows. This combination denotes Siva, the deity representative of destruction and regeneration, for the cow is a symbol of production.

Whenever the umbrella features prominently in sepulchral architecture, it also represents, to a varying extent, the heavens to which the deceased has ascended. On the west coast of India there are many examples of the tomb termed *Koda-kallu*, or Umbrella Stone, so-called because of its shape, which closed the entrance to the underground tomb and honoured the deceased person by showing that he had been judged worthy of a celestial afterlife. The name *Koda-kallu* is also given to a similar monument found in the same area, where the stone is perched on one or more crudely hewn rocks. These appear to be memorials to the dead rather than sepulchres, for archaeologists have found nothing underneath them. About a thousand years ago, umbrellas of stone were erected in temple courtyards around Bangalore as memorials to notable people who merited something more substantial than the wooden umbrellas sometimes placed near tombs; similar stones have been found over a thousand miles away in Burma.

Many Indian tribes of differing religions preserve this umbrella-fetish in their burial rites, notably the Kotas of the Nilgiris, low-caste Hindus who act as blacksmiths and musicians to the neighbouring tribes. When one of their number dies his brethren construct a fantastic funeral car several storeys high, which forms the centre-piece of the procession. A ceremonial umbrella is included, and in modern times smart utility models are also fixed to the car. The corpse itself is protected by a canopy, called a *pandal* in Southern India. The custom as a whole dates back to at least the fourth century after Christ.

The most widespread use of the umbrella as a funeral symbol is on the 'stupa', or Buddhist burial monument and relic shrine, known to the Sinhalese as *dagabas* and formerly termed 'topes' by Anglo-Indians. The Sinhalese chronicle known as the *Mahavamsa*, in describing the building and dedication of the *Mahathupa* or Great Stupa in about 77 BC, tells how King

Dutthagamani dedicated his own state umbrella to the stupa with the words: 'Thrice over do I dedicate my kingdom to the saviour of the world, the divine teacher, the bearer of the triple canopy: the canopy of the heavenly host, the canopy of mortals, and the canopy of eternal emancipation.' The royal umbrella remained on the stupa for a week, after which it was replaced by a wooden model which was lavishly ornamented by subsequent rulers.

A. H. Longhurst, former Archaeological Commissioner for Ceylon, has suggested that it was in the reign of the Indian king, Asoka, (who established Buddhism as the main religion of the people in the third century before Christ) that the umbrella became closely connected with the stupa. From about this period a model of brass and stone, variously known as the *chatra-vali*, *chatra* or *chatta* (the latter being the Indian name for the common sunshade) was carefully placed in position on the monument so that it was impossible to meddle with the tee—the receptacle for the valuable offerings—without it being dislodged. Thus the umbrella was a symbol of royal protection and approval. Longhurst also records how the ensuing use of multi-canopied umbrellas went through several stages of evolution:

> In the beautiful Sanchi bas-reliefs we have many representations of stupas surmounted by single-, double-, and triple-canopied umbrellas, together with superimposed groups of umbrellas numbering from three to five; but they have not as yet been conventionalised so as to produce the pyramid of superimposed discs which subsequently came to be recognised as the symbol of the whole. Thus we have the primary idea of the accumulated honour of the pyramid of stone or metal discs, which eventually had such a profound influence on Buddhist architecture, culminating in the many-storeyed pagodas of China and Japan.[3]

Eventually the groups of umbrellas forming the top part of the stupa came to be represented by solid stone spires with small serrations down the side, but both this form and the intermediary stages retained the same significance. Dietrich Seckel explains this symbolism in a passage in his book *The Art of Buddhism*:

> The terraces, tiers and umbrellas on the stupa, and the storeys and rings on top of the pagoda represent the cosmic spheres superimposed upon one another: the spheres of deities and Bodhisattvas, which must

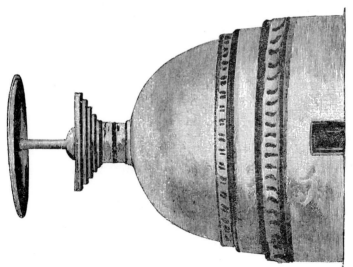

Indian stupas showing the umbrella finial in an early form (*left*), and in its evolved state as a series of discs

be interpreted as planes of cosmic existence, and at the same time as *bhumi*: stages of consciousness, meditation, maturation, and enlightenment; seen in the temporal sense, they are successive stages on the path to redemption leading ultimately beyond the limits of time and space. In this way the stupa or pagoda takes over the ancient Indian cosmological interpretation of the world mountain Sumeru, which is related to the widely disseminated image of the cosmic pillar or tree—the latter, again, is identical with the Tree of Enlightenment. This cosmic axis . . . in some buildings . . . is . . . represented by the mast with umbrellas. On account of the importance attached to this symbolism, when building a pagoda, great care was taken to retain the centre pillar.[4]

In India, and indeed the whole of Asia, the widespread use of the umbrella may originally have been due to its religious significance, but its importance extends far beyond the limits of pious reverence. Indian potentates, for instance, have been eager to employ it as an indication of their high rank and some have even made it their exclusive prerogative. Such a one was the Great Mogul of whom it was written: 'of kittasols of state, for to shadow him, there be twenty. None in his empire dareth in any sort have any of these carried for his shadow but himself.'[5]

Before the British conquest of India, Europeans who unwittingly carried umbrellas on state occasions were liable to give grave offence and even to find themselves in some danger from natives jealous of their rulers' privileges. On the other hand, when David Dyce Sombre was adopted as the son and heir of the Begum of Sirdanah (in Hindustan), he was permitted to take the royal umbrella as part of his crest. Thus it featured in the coat of arms he used in Britain, where he was elected a member of Parliament, ejected from his seat for bribery, and certified as insane, before dying in 1851.

The rajahs of the state of Cochin even included the symbol in the paper on which their postage stamps were printed, a large umbrella forming the watermark of each sheet. Later on, each stamp had a small umbrella outlined in its paper. Other rulers have been at pains to evolve their own particular designs of parasol. A Maharajah of Nagpur once owned a magnificent model which had sixteen ribs covered with silk and decorated with gold and silver ornaments; the handle and stick were silver-plated. In the mid-nineteenth century, the Maharajah of Dholpur's model was of the unusual bell-type, with the cover suspended from the stick, a design possibly chosen for its originality, though a similar type had been previously known in China.

When foreign princes and rulers visit India, they are traditionally accompanied in their travels throughout the land by one or more ceremonial umbrellas, which proclaim their rank in the eyes of the people. Many of the British royal family have been honoured in this way; when the Prince of Wales toured the country in 1877 he was often escorted by a golden parasol, and returned home with a collection of twenty magnificent umbrellas. The costliest came from the Begum of Ode and was made of blue silk, stitched with gold thread and covered with red pearls. Other items in this splendid array included a state umbrella from Indore, in the shape of a mushroom, and the sunshade of the Queen of Lucknow, in blue satin stitched with gold, and covered with fine pearls. The coverings were many and varied, from gilt paper to the feathers of rare birds, but most of the frames had the same long handles of gold and silver inlaid in painted wood and beautifully carved ivory. (A few years before the prince's visit, in 1874, certain belligerent rulers entitled to such grand sunshades had taken advantage of the privilege by importing packages labelled 'Umbrellas', perhaps hoping that the officials would suppose they were handling state regalia and would let them pass without inspection. But, in fact, the authorities at Tanna discovered the packages contained fifteen double-barrelled guns and 175 lb of powder.)

The makers of the royal umbrellas, who were not necessarily natives but sometimes Europeans from leading firms in London and Paris, had long lost sight of the detailed rules given in the *Yukti kalapataru* for the proportions and manufacture of all types of umbrella. That termed the *kanaka-danda*, with frame of sandalwood mounted in gold and with a pure white gold-fringed cover, was the chosen design for a noble. A prince was entitled to a *pratapa*, with a blue, gold-fringed cloth, and a king would have been honoured to received a *prasada*, with stick of choice wood, ribs of selected bamboo and a cover of scarlet cloth. But the most important of all models was the *nava-danda*, which was reserved for the highest state occasions—coronations, royal marriages and suchlike. The frame was of pure gold fitted with a handle consisting of a ruby with a diamond knob; its cover was of the choicest silk, fringed with thirty-two looped strings of pearls, with thirty-two pearls on each string—over a thousand pearls in all.

In the India of today an umbrella is often carried simply to enhance the dignity of someone who might otherwise pass unnoticed, and as far back as 1687 it was decided that the aldermen of Madras Corporation (a mixture of Indians and English freemen) might have 'kettysols' carried over them to emphasise their authority—'kettysol' being one of many variations of the Portuguese word *quitasol*, or sunshade. The Tamil people are especially aware of the umbrella's symbolism, and, with the speakers of Telegu, have this proverb: 'When fortune smiles on a mean person he orders an umbrella to be brought at midnight' (so anxious is he to advertise his new position).

The umbrella features prominently in countless Indian festivals and celebrations, such as the *Kudaikuttu* or Umbrella Dance, in which Sub'rahmanya, the god of war, slays the demon Surapadmasura and performs his own dance of triumph. One of the most important figures in the procession represents the god's umbrella-bearer who prances around with a parasol—more legend than religion this. The models used on ceremonial occasions either have a domed cover, or else a flat top, rather like a wheel. The frames are wooden, covered with coloured cloth or silk, with a fringe, and sometimes topped by a brass or copper ornament. The covers measure 5 ft or more in diameter, and the poles are about 8 ft long. These designs have changed little over the years as both types are shown in second-century sculptures at Gandhara.

The Santals, a hill tribe from near Calcutta, are on record as having had a spring-time custom of erecting a garlanded pole topped with an umbrella, around which they danced in a form of worship.[6] Their 'pole' may well have been a denuded sal tree such as features in a similar celebration, the *Ch'hatparab* or Umbrella Feast, held by the Dravidian-speaking tribes of North India when they need abundant rain for their rice crop. F. B.

A sal tree topped by an umbrella, worshipped by the
Santals in the nineteenth century

Bradley-Birt describes this further variation on the fertility
theme in his book *Indian Upland*:

> A long lithe sal tree shorn of its branches supports the smallest of
> umbrellas roughly made of gaudy tinsel, and together, amidst the ex-
> cited shouts of the celebrants, they are raised aloft until, standing per-
> pendicularly, the sal trunk is fixed firmly in the ground. As it slowly
> settles into place, the people, gathering up handfuls of dust and earth,
> pelt the umbrella with loud cries and much laughter, dancing around it
> the while as round a maypole, while the men turn somersaults and
> perform wonders of athletics and acrobatic skills. Copious drinking of
> rice beer brings the feast to a close.[7]

In many parts of India an umbrella is prominent in wedding
processions, notably those of the Hindus. Usually an attendant
is responsible for the large ceremonial umbrella, but in the north,
and also in Nepal, the bridegroom himself may carry a normal-
sized, lavishly-decorated model. The reason most commonly
given for the umbrella's presence is that it lends the groom, and

the occasion, dignity, but it also has ulterior significance, perhaps long-forgotten, as an invocation for a fruitful marriage.

The honorific parasol was by no means exclusive to the natives of India and engravings made by the Dutchman, Jan Huyghen van Linschoten, in the 1580s show that the Portuguese colonists in Goa, on the western coast, were seldom without protection from the sun. They were frequently escorted by servants staggering under heavy parasols which seem unnecessarily cumbersome compared with the contemporary *aftab-giv* or utility umbrella, a flat disc mounted on a rod. When at the Goanese slave market, for instance, Europeans would walk around inspecting slaves or goods, then perhaps take refreshment at a table, all the while attended by a parasol-bearer. The market people provided a stand for temporarily discarded umbrellas—or perhaps even furnished umbrellas to those of their patrons who found the sun hotter than expected.

Doubtless some protection from the sun was necessary, but the colonists obviously had adopted umbrellas as status symbols, Goa being a paradise for the parvenu where most of the work was done by slaves. Here, common soldiers were able to assume high-sounding titles, and impoverished noblemen congregated together in boarding-houses to subscribe towards a cloak, umbrella and manservant so they could take it in turns to promenade the streets fashionably attired and suitably escorted.

Contemporary prints, such as those made by the De Bry brothers in the 1590s, satirise these habits under titles like 'How common Portuguese appear in the streets'. These show pompous merchants enjoying the protection of *tiresols* or *tirasols*, as they termed the sunshades. One engraving, by Linschoten, features a small ship carrying merchandise and manned by a score or more of native rowers, whose Portuguese supervisor carries a parasol in one hand and a staff in the other. In the stern of the vessel stands another, more conically-shaped, umbrella, temporarily discarded.

Portuguese women in India also adopted the umbrella, and would not venture out without an escort of slaves, one of whom bore a shade over his mistress to protect her from the sun and to emphasise her prestige. When these women later returned to

Portugal, they took their umbrellas with them and soon established them as a fashionable custom.

Portuguese seamen also included the umbrella in their equipment when they travelled further eastwards, beyond India, on their trading voyages, and found it useful, in ceremonial or as a gift to local potentates, in almost every region they visited. In 1543, one of their China-bound ships was driven off-course into Japanese waters and its commander forced to go ashore to make his peace with the authorities; he was accompanied by a bearer with a furled parasol, which, as soon as he had landed, was opened out and held over him to emphasise his rank.

In fact, in those countries on the other side of the Bay of Bengal, to the east of India, the umbrella had been known for many centuries before the Europeans' arrival. In this area both Chinese and Indian influences have been evident in its use, but little is known about the earliest models, their origins and employment, other than that they were widely regarded as a privilege of the highest rank.

Certain it is, however, that it was the eastward spread of Buddhism that firmly established the umbrella as a religious object, and as such it has retained great importance in Eastern Asia down to this century. In Tibetan temples large silk parasols or *gdugs* are still hung above altars. In East Pakistan, in the area around Chittagong, the parasol has long been regarded as an ecclesiastical privilege; for the *Boro-Sahib*, chief priest of the sect of Mughs, it was his principal emblem of power, whilst the senior cleric of each of the various districts was also entitled to bear it.

Of all the Asian countries, Burma and Siam have shown most regard for the umbrella as a symbol of sovereignty. One Burmese king even chose his successor by placing his umbrella in the midst of his five sons and praying it might fall towards the most worthy. Prince Oksana was thus chosen, and, when he eventually came to the throne in 1211, he was known as Tilominlo—'the king whom the umbrella placed on the throne'. The proud title of the erstwhile ruler of Ava, the ancient capital of the Burmese empire, was 'King of the White Elephants and Lord of the Twenty-Four Umbrellas'. In December 1769, a treaty between

Burma and China referred to 'the Sun-descended King, the lord who rules over the multitude of umbrella-bearing chiefs in the Western Kingdom, and the Master of the Golden Palace of China, who rules over a multitude of umbrella-bearing chiefs in the Great Eastern Kingdom'.

The king's personal attendants included forty bearers of the royal white umbrellas, and these men took turns of duty at the palace in rotation. The white umbrella was sacred to royalty, and on state occasions the king was accompanied by eight models, each of which was about 15 ft high and 6 ft wide and had a handle richly decorated with gold-encrusted gems. As in India, many foreigners got into trouble for using white shades against the sun and so infringing the royal prerogative, an offence classed as high treason and punishable by death.

The chief queen was allotted only one of these white umbrellas, and was therefore less privileged than the sacred white elephant, which was honoured by some half-dozen parasols and was even entitled to a royal funeral under one. People less important than the king, queen or white elephant were permitted golden-coloured umbrellas, the crown prince being escorted by eight of these. The king decided how many models other relatives, high-ranking officers and particular favourites might be allowed, and it was counted a great honour when he accorded the British resident, Colonel Fytche, and his wife, two golden umbrellas each in 1867.

This gave the couple the same status as the six Buddhist priests who had arrived in Amarapura in 1802 after a long journey from Ceylon to be ordained into the highest order of their faith. Extraordinary pomp marked their arrival in the city, where they were placed in golden howdahs on the stateliest elephants, each priest being escorted by two servants carrying superb golden umbrellas. (Incidentally, it is curious that the umbrella, so much a symbol of pomp and rank, should also be used by some Buddhist monks to divert attention from themselves. When in the public eye, they sometimes carry large scallop-shaped models of palm-leaves to hide their faces from passers-by.)

The Burmese decorated their war-elephants with multi-tiered umbrellas, which no doubt looked very picturesque, but must

Burmese state umbrellas (nineteenth century)

have presented some problems in a high wind! Their sometime enemies, the Siamese, had a similar custom, and indeed, till the late nineteenth century, both nations used umbrellas in much the same ways, particularly in the royal households. But in 1885, the Burmese Alaunghaya dynasty ended, with King Theebaw's surrender to the British, and then came a change in Burmese umbrellas. The beautiful regal models disappeared, and the colourful silk parasols, hitherto produced locally, were temporarily discarded for low-quality British umbrellas in sombre black.

But in Siam, the immaculate royal umbrellas continue to this day to be an important part of the Siamese state regalia. In the royal throne room may still be seen an identical arrangement to that noted in 1687 by Simon de la Loubère, the French envoy to the Siamese court, who remarked that the only furniture in the

king's hall of audience consisted of three umbrellas, a central one
of nine tiers flanked by a pair with seven shades each. He
assumed, correctly enough, that the umbrella in Siam had the
same significance as the canopy in his homeland.[8] At this same
period, the Talapoins, a cult of Siamese monks, had umbrellas
made of palm-leaves folded so that the stems formed the handles.
A century before, an Englishman, Ralph Fitch, mentioned that
the 'Tallipoies' carried 'a great broad sombrero or shadow in
their hands to defend them in the summer from the sun and in
the winter from the rain'.[9]

Some of the modern, gorgeously-bejewelled, state umbrellas
are equipped with heavy shades of the richest embroidery, and
encrusted with so many precious stones and gold ornaments that
several men are required to carry them. Umbrellas as symbols of
dignity are also prominent in the Siamese state jewels, notably
in the Collar of the Royal Order of the White Elephant of Siam,
which is reserved exclusively for crowned heads and their heirs
and which has been conferred on such rulers as Queen Victoria,
Edward VII and an emperor of Germany. The central ornament
on the collar represents a white elephant bearing a relic shrine.
On each side stand two pyramids of nine umbrellas—the highest
honour possible. Thus the accumulated dignity of thirty-six
umbrellas is conferred on the sacred beast and its burden.

As was the custom in Burma, the King of Siam may present
umbrellas to his favourites, who gauge their popularity by the
trimmings, and it is usual for visiting dignitaries to be so
honoured. When Mrs Jacqueline Kennedy, widow of the American President, visited the country in 1967, she was accorded the
privilege of the ceremonial umbrella.

Utility and costume parasols have never been as popular in
Siam as in neighbouring countries, despite the fact that whiteness
of the skin is regarded as a hall-mark of beauty. In the market
places, however, large sunshades protect the wares on display,
and it is here that many of the hand-made, personal models are
produced, with the bamboo frames, skilfully fitted together
without glue or nails, and covered in hand-made paper dyed a
rich red. Some proud owners so prize their umbrellas that they
protect them under their clothing during a downpour.

Siamese umbrellas (seventeenth century), presented by
the king to his favourites

In Cambodia, Laos and Viet-Nam the umbrella has always
been used in much the same way as in Siam. In Annam, now part
of South Viet-Nam, the ceremonial umbrella in the nineteenth
century was of black and red varnished paper on an elaborate
bamboo frame-work. When the king rode forth on his elephant
he was usually accompanied by a servant with a three-tiered
model. Annamite mandarins were also entitled to have umbrellas
held over them, though the permissible number of tiers varied
according to the district and their rank; at Hué they were
allowed only one, but in other provinces the number was greater.

The present-day Kings of Laos and Cambodia both perpetuate
the centuries-old custom of their countries by retaining their
royal models, and one of the most spectacular displays of parasols
in the twentieth century occurred at the obsequies of King
Sisavang Vong of Laos in April 1961. His funeral carriage was
both preceded and followed by white shades, and the gilded
funeral pyre surrounded by a dozen seven-tiered umbrellas.

There is good reason to believe that it was from this part of South-East Asia that the honorific parasol spread across the Atlantic to America centuries before the voyage of Columbus. Quinatzin IV, fourteenth-century king of the Chechemecas of Mexico, is said to have progressed under 'an umbrella which was carried by four others' (probably a canopy) shortly after his accession. The Utlatlans had a tier system to denote rank: four tiers indicated a king, three his heir, two the chief captain, and one his lieutenant.

Dr Gordon Elkholm, when Associate Curator of Archaeology at the American Museum of Natural History, reckoned the parasol to be an important link between the American Maya and the Asians, providing evidence of contact between the old and new worlds long before the arrival of Spanish influences. Having considered other similarities, he felt that:

> . . . in reading descriptions of the palace and court of the Aztec Emperor, anyone familiar with South-East Asia cannot fail to be reminded of the courts of Burma, Siam and Cambodia . . . the possibility of attributing Hindu-Buddhist influence in Mexico . . . indicates the existence of some kind of two-way traffic between South-East Asia and America in ancient times.[10]

Though the Siamese type of umbrella may have spread half-way aross the world to America, it does not seem to have reached neighbouring Malaya, where the Chinese are generally credited with the introduction of the single-tiered yellow umbrella as a symbol of royalty. Several Malay sultans, having married Chinese princesses, took to using somewhat plain umbrellas on official occasions. Certainly utility models in this part of the world are based on Chinese design, with opaque oiled paper stretched over bamboo ribs. They are lighter, but neither as well made nor as pretty as those in the Japanese style. Even so, the most humble models have long been considered important by the natives.

In the 1850s J. D. Vaughan noted that, in the Straits Settlements:

> In the country, hundreds of Chinese may be seen trudging along with umbrellas spread, although it may be cloudy weather and not a vestige of the sun to be seen. Late in the evening too the umbrella is carefully

Page 53 (above) Shan chiefs escorted by honorific parasols, India, 1911;
(below) King George V and Queen Mary accompanied by a state parasol during
their visit to India, 1911. Others of the royal party have to provide their own
shade

Page 54 Morning ritual in the Ganges at Benares

kept open and held over the head. The height of respectability appears
to be a clean white *baju* [a garment] and silk umbrella. The writer has
often been amused to see a well-known low fellow step into the witness box of a court with his umbrella and white *baju*, borrowed
doubtless to impress the lookers-on with his respectability.[11]

Because such pretentiousness attaches to the umbrella, it is the
custom in many parts of Malaya to leave it outside when entering
a mine, the natives believing that anyone so presumptuous as to
take it inside, even closed, would offend the dignity of the
guardian spirits. Incidentally, Malaya is yet another part of the
world where an umbrella is held over the bridegroom's head at a
wedding; smart black umbrellas, inscribed with Chinese characters, are also featured at funerals.

In Indonesia, the cult of the umbrella is not now so noticeable
as in other parts of Asia, though the honorific parasol does
feature in some of the older sculptures, probably as a result of
Buddhist influence. When the Dutch first reached the area in
1595, they were obviously impressed by the number of utility
sunshades and depicted these in many illustrations of the time.
Other nationalities, notably the Portuguese and English, noticed
the ceremonial parasols, and referred to them in accounts of their
voyages.

Many Indonesian monarchs of this period had umbrellas held
over them, the kings of Bali, Ternate and Bantam all attaching
great significance to this sign of prestige; the sovereign of
Bantam expected his presents to be protected by 'a rich Tierasoll'.
In Java, the various ranks of chiefs were at one time denoted by
umbrellas of six different colours, a custom which, for all its
convenience, has been seldom met with, though some countries
have reserved a certain colour for royalty. This again suggests the
influence of China, where great attention was once paid to the
colour-scheme of a man's umbrella.

In Borneo, the graves of chiefs have been ornamented with
seven-tiered umbrellas, whilst Dusun tribesmen still place an open
umbrella of ordinary design above a wooden shrine. They are
said to believe that it will keep the dead man's spirit dry but
there may well be a deeper significance, bearing in mind the
widespread funeral symbolism of the umbrella. The island's

D

rulers have also used an umbrella as part of their insignia of office, and the Sultan of Brunei still has a smart white-tasselled model held over him on official occasions. An umbrella canopy is also a feature of the royal arms of Brunei.

New Guinea's proximity to Indonesia might have been expected to have led to the adoption of the usual umbrella customs in that island (the seventeenth-century ruler of Ternate, less than 300 miles to the east, laid great store on his royal umbrella), but the natives do not seem to have adopted umbrellas to any extent. Only one relevant practice has been noted, and this on the north-west coast, where a woman was not allowed to leave her house for some time after she had borne a child. When she finally did so she had to cover her head with a hood or umbrella to prevent the sun shining on her, the belief being that without this precaution one of her male relatives might die. This superstition is similar to that of the Dyaks of Borneo who think that an umbrella placed over the head protects the bearer from evil.

The experience of two missionaries at Katan, on the south coast of the island, in 1871, certainly suggests that the natives were unaware of any special symbolism attaching to the umbrella, if indeed they had ever previously seen one:

> As at Sabai, the umbrellas were objects of special interest, so much so that we could not resist the temptation to leave them with the people. One was given to the chief, and the other to another man of importance, and the demonstrations that followed the same gifts were amusing indeed. One grand difficulty, however, soon checked their joy, the umbrellas were opened and could not be shut again, although we had repeatedly opened and shut them amid roars of laughter. At length, one fortunate fellow discovered the secret, and was rewarded by the loud acclamations of the bystanders.[12]

In modern times the natives have maintained their interest in the umbrella, but treat it more as a gimmick than as a symbol. The inhabitants of New Guinea are perhaps the fiercest-looking people on earth, yet even they do not look quite so terrifying when walking under a gamp!

The New Guinean's lack of appreciation for the umbrella is the more puzzling for the fact that some of their fellow Melanesians formerly used it in a religious role some 1,800 miles away in Fiji.

They regarded it as the privilege of the king and his two high priests, who were shaded by models made of cabbage leaves, a rare commodity in the islands. At one religious festival at Somo-Somo, on the isle of Taveuni, the shade-bearer, the *Linga Vui*, danced around the other natives with a sunshade of palm-leaves. Captain Cook also, in the course of one of his voyages, is said to have noted the use of umbrellas by South Sea islanders. Both instances may tentatively be attributed to widely diffused influences from the Malay archipelago.

In modern times, of course, white men have introduced the utility sunshade to those natives of the New Hebrides and Solomon Islands who worked on estates in Fiji and Australia. On returning home, the most prized of their acquisitions would be multi-coloured umbrellas, proud evidence of their advanced state of civilisation!

It has already been told in Chapter 1 how the umbrella was used in China from very early times, with little apparent connection with Western practice. In fact, it was not until the seventh century and the establishment of Buddhism that outside influences began to affect Chinese umbrella customs. For some time previously, information about the religion had been finding its way eastward; about AD 520, Hwei Sang had taken home with him copper models of the great stupa at Peshawar, in what is now Pakistan. In those days the stupa finial had thirteen superimposed umbrellas on an iron rod 30 ft high. The traveller Hiuen Tsang, a century later, was also impressed by the same stupa, which contained relics of Buddha himself, and was regarded as one of the wonders of the world. By Hiuen Tsang's time, the number of umbrellas had been increased to twenty-five, and these were now copper-gilt. The stupa in general, and the Peshawar example in particular, was the inspiration for the Chinese pagoda, which became a prominent feature of early Chinese-Buddhist temple architecture. Both, as we have seen, represented the cosmos, and in the course of the stupa's transformation into the pagoda umbrellas continued to be represented in an abstruse way as storeys and finial rings.

Very soon, Buddhist and Chinese umbrellas became closely identified with each other, so that it is often hard to distinguish the place of origin of a custom. But it was probably due to Buddhist influence that umbrellas began to feature at funerals in China, though personal models had been interred with the deceased for some centuries previously. The type used was indicative of the rank of the dead man, the corpse of a mandarin being accompanied to the grave by an umbrella of blue and white silk, embroidered with yellow dragons; minor officials had to make do with cloth instead of silk. When a wealthy man died, open umbrellas of paper and tinsel were placed beside his coffin. Thirty-five days after death, the daughter of the deceased, or some other close relative, would burn an umbrella of red paper on a framework of sorghum cane, together with imitation paper.

The rules of umbrella etiquette in China varied from period to period. Prior to the tenth century, blue and green silk parasols were reserved for princes of imperial rank; later the privilege was extended to ladies of the palace on their visits to town. An edict of 1012 stipulated that only members of the imperial family might be allowed parasols, but this was soon ignored. Thereafter the regulations became more precise; in the Ming dynasty (1368–1644), for example, the governor-general of a province, or any military officer of high rank, was heralded by two great red silk umbrellas. The four highest ranks of mandarins were entitled to umbrellas of black *lo* (a type of Chinese gauze) with red silk lining and three flounces, and one may guess that this variation on the tier system was of Buddhist origin. The lesser nobility were allowed but two flounces which, incidentally, should not be confused with tiers and storeys. The latter were popular in Siam, each tier usually being separate from the others, whereas flounces overlapped one another.

Gentlemen commoners of the two highest ranks had red umbrellas surmounted by a gourd-shaped knob of block tin; the next two degrees had the knob made of wood, painted red. The fifth rank could carry only a model of blue cloth, with a red-painted knob and two flounces. Ordinary people were not allowed umbrellas covered with cloth or silk, and used instead models of stout paper, which were quite adequate for keeping off sun or rain, if commanding less prestige. Some idea of their intrinsic value is afforded by the fact that in 1386 these utility models cost the same as ten writing brushes or a hundred peaches and pears!

Later on, a red silk or satin umbrella, termed the *Wang-ming-san*, or Umbrella of Ten Thousand People, was sometimes presented to a popular official to mark his executive authority and as a tribute to his rank and the respect in which he was held. Its pole was 9 ft high, surmounted by a gilt knob, and the cover was often inscribed in gilt letters with the names of the principal donors. Such an umbrella was seldom given to a foreigner, though Sir Arthur Kennedy, governor of Hong Kong, received one when his term of office expired in 1877.

The very highest honours in umbrellas were, of course, enjoyed by the emperor of China. On ordinary occasions he would be accompanied by twelve umbrella-bearers and twenty-four fan-bearers. But when Ki-tsiang, T'ung chi was married at Peking in 1872 the occasion was marked by a spectacular pro-

Procession of state umbrellas at the Emperor of China's marriage, Peking, 1872

cession in which almost every participant carried a banner or
very tall triple-flounced umbrella, of various colours and embroidered with dragons and phoenixes. At the end of the procession came the Imperial Canopy, or Yellow Dragon Umbrella
which, when not in use, was jealously guarded in the emperor's
palace. It was accounted a great honour when one imperial ruler
extended his privilege of the Yellow Umbrella to certain Llama
monasteries in North China and Mongolia.

Not only was the umbrella important to potentates but also to
the ordinary Chinese who revered the umbrella no less than did
his social superiors. Charles Ray has told the story of a Chinese
convert to Christianity who read in the New Testament: 'Who-
soever will come after Me, let him deny himself and take up his
cross and follow Me.' His umbrella being the possession he most
valued and esteemed, he took it with him to the mission.[13]

Although the symbolism and high status once attaching to the
umbrella no longer prevail to anything like the same extent as in
the past, utility models are more popular than ever in China
today. It is quite common to see two men precariously mounted
on a single bicycle, the rear rider holding a parasol over the front
one. Often, too, an umbrella is held aloft when there is no need
for it, or when it would be more convenient to dispense with it,
so important is it to the morale of the Oriental.

The cheaper umbrellas are still made of paper manufactured
from cotton rags, whilst the better models utilise paper made of
the bark bast of the paper mulberry. The bast is mixed with a
little bamboo bark and boiled in water to which chalk and rice
stubble have been added. The result is a strong paper which
needs considerable effort to tear. The covers are painted and
lacquered, and sometimes decorated with the maxims of Con-
fucius, though from the 1960s the sayings of that famous philoso-
pher have sometimes taken second place to those of Mao-Tse
Tung. Westerners have been surprised by the number of ribs
fitted to some Chinese models, which can be as high as forty-two,
though in the twelfth century the author of the *Cheu-li*, an
authoritative work on umbrella manufacture, recommended
twenty-eight as being preferable.

The thirteenth-century encyclopaedist, Vincent of Beauvais,

mentioned that the Tartars, then under Chinese influence, favoured the *tentoriolum* or 'little tent', which they always used when riding. These were customarily carried by the principal men and their wives, and often had handles covered with jewels. In the previous century, every free Tartar soldier had to provide an umbrella as part of his equipment. Whether it was for practical use or had a religious origin we do not know, but the picture it conjures up is oddly at variance with our Western image of the fierce Tartar.

In the late thirteenth century, Marco Polo recorded that Kublai Khan awarded each of his most important barons, who commanded at least 100,000 men, an inscribed golden tablet, and, as a handier token of power, a small umbrella to be carried by the privileged leader.[14] A few years later, Mar Yahbhallaha III, a Chinese monk of the Nestorian church, journeyed through much the same country as Polo, and received several parasols from various rulers. A Syrian manuscript records that when the Mongol ruler, King Abhgha, wished to confirm the monk's position as Patriarch of the Church:

> . . . he gave him also a parasol (*shather*) which is called in Mongolian *sukor*, and this is raised up above the heads of kings and queens and their children, and it is sufficient to keep away from them the strength of the sun and rain; but on most occasions parasols are spread over them to do them honour.[15]

Another rather mysterious tribe which favoured the umbrella were the Calmucs, in whose country an interesting sculpture was discovered in October 1721, and subsequently investigated by the French scholar and archaeologist, Father Montfaucon. Montfaucon was told by M. de Schumacker, library-keeper to the Czar of Russia, that 'the Calmucs are Tartars under the protection of her Czarian Majesty. They inhabit the country between Siberia and the Caspian Sea to the East of the Volga'. Such an area would include most of present-day Russia, and in fact the Calmucs originated in Mongolia and Tibet, but settled northwest of the Caspian Sea, while a few of their number made their homes in Kirgizia, on the Chinese border. M. de Schumacker wrote of the sculpture as being:

... a horseman, with stirrups, which we never find the horsemen of
the ancients have . . . Behind the horseman, a naked boy holds an
umbrella to shade his master from the heat of the sun. Before the
horseman, this is a very little man, naked, he seems old, and holds in
his hand a human heart; this is some mystery.[16]

At the time this statuette was discovered the Calmucs were
Buddhists, but they did not adopt this religion until the sixteenth and seventeenth centuries, whereas the umbrella, with its
slanted handle, appears to be of earlier date. Perhaps they
borrowed it from the Persians, from whom, long ago, they were
separated only by the Caucasus mountains. It is possible also
that they adopted it from Mongolia where, as in other countries
to the north of the Himalaya and Hindu Kush mountain ranges,
there have undoubtedly been umbrella customs which are only
hinted at in the records of western travellers.

In Japan, the umbrella's importance was recognised from an
early period, for tombs of the fifth century AD contain sepulchral
sculptures of clay called *haniwa*, which sometimes represent
kinugasa, or sunshades, which probably had bamboo handles and
frames, filled out with some textile, leaves or feathers, and were
status symbols to emphasis the rank of the deceased. Replicas,
not originals, were placed in tombs, perhaps because the
originals, being part of some official regalia, were handed down
from generation to generation.

Umbrellas feature in a representation of a village on the back
of a magnificent bronze mirror found in the fourth-century
Takarazuka tomb at Kawai village, in the Nara prefecture. It has
been suggested that the scene shows the lull before a storm, and
that the umbrellas are signs of approaching bad weather. It is thus
possible that in the Far East the early umbrella was also a rain-
symbol and similarly associated with fertility as it was thousands
of miles away to the west.[17]

Whilst the original use of the umbrella in Japan was no doubt
influenced by the Chinese, the advent of Buddhism made comparatively little impact on its symbolic use. It was not until the
seventh century AD that the religion was adopted in Japan,
following Prince Shotuku Taishi's invitation to Korean Buddhists
to come and establish it in his country. These missionaries

brought with them their religion's own form of architecture, in which, by this time, the umbrella was seldom represented in its basic and obvious form, though finials of multiple shades were sometimes placed on the tops of buildings. So, instead, the Japanese came to use overhanging eaves and pyramids of discs to portray the heavens symbolised by the original umbrella-motif.

However, the Japanese continued to employ the ceremonial umbrella for many centuries, though without endowing it with anything like as much mystique as did their Chinese neighbours. But its importance was sufficient for differentiation to be made between the *higasa*, made of plain paper over split bamboo, and the *komori-gasa*, or European umbrella. The *naga-e* was held over noblemen when riding, whereas the *tsumaori-gasa* was the emblem of officials, priests and court nobles. Perhaps it was under his *tsumaori-gasa* that Hideyoshi was sitting in the sixteenth century, when, tradition says, his enemy, the warrior Shibata, fired at long range an arrow which split the pole of his umbrella.

Today, ceremonial models are infrequently seen, and then mostly in pageantry or in the less advanced areas, such as the island of Hekura where a tall red parasol is carried in processions held during late August to mark the end of the fishing season.

The umbrella has a unique place in Japanese art which, over the centuries, has featured a wide variety of utility-type models. These frequently afford some special significance to paintings, with well-known characters like Feng-tsze using one for a boat, Wang Chu receiving a letter from a flying umbrella, and the notorious Sadakuro clutching a dilapidated old umbrella as he tries to murder Yoichebe.[18] Furthermore, artists have been able to exploit the parasol itself, using it as a form of heraldic device to denote which particular school its geisha-bearer might come from; it is a popular custom for such girls to dance with suitably painted sunshades and fans in Tokyo tea-houses.

It seems probable that the Japanese acquired the technique of umbrella manufacture from the Chinese, and the work of both nationalities is even today very similar, though one or two old Japanese makers still like to make an entire frame from one length of bamboo stick and observe the traditional preference for florally ornamented covers. In recent years Japanese manufacturers have tended to specialise in the production of low-priced models similar to European makes, and have established a strong grip—and in some places a stranglehold—on the international market.

3 The Umbrella in Africa

WHEREAS IN ASIA one cannot be sure in which direction the use of the umbrella spread, in Africa it is most probable that it passed from Egypt along the coasts of the Mediterranean and Red Sea, then down the western and eastern shores of the continent. Three areas in particular, Ethiopia, Morocco and West Africa, were notable for its enthusiastic adoption, each in its own manner, and it is in these three places that the cult of the umbrella is still strongest today.

In Ethiopia, both the emperor and empress are entitled to a smart state umbrella, a custom dating back at least 2,500 years, when it is recorded that King Nastasen was enthroned under one. About AD 1600 Manoel de Almeida mentioned, probably inaccurately, the royal 'silk umbrella which came . . . from India' and referred to an official, known as *Arnes*, who was responsible for the royal umbrella at coronations. Certainly two umbrellas were conspicuous when Haile Selassie was crowned in 1930, one being small and decorated with fringes, the other far larger but somewhat plain. Two days afterwards, when the emperor and his wife, attired in full regalia save for their crowns, visited the chief metropolitan churches of Addis Ababa, an extra seat had to be attached to their car so that two parasol-bearers could accompany them.

Ethiopia must also be the only country were the umbrella still features prominently in Christian ceremony, the Church there having strong associations with the Copts of Egypt, from whom this particular usage might have derived. In 1209, Kilas, Bishop of Tua, came from Alexandria to assume the supremacy of the Abyssinian church, and on arrival was met by 'the king's nobles',

who conducted him to his quarters under an umbrella of cloth
of gold. (When the nineteenth-century orientalist, Prisse
d'Avennes, wished to photograph the Coptic Patriarch at
Alexandria, he was allowed to do so only on condition that he
included in the picture the open parasol which the Patriarch had
received from the Khedive.)

In a fresco in Old Trinity Church at Addis Ababa which
depicts the Burial of the Virgin Mary, two sunshades are prominent in the background, and several old manuscripts show
monarchs such as David, Solomon and Constantine escorted by
umbrellas. Their inclusion is by no means anachronistic and can
be attributed to the artists' intention to symbolise the sovereignty
or saintliness of the figures.

Ceremonial umbrellas also dominate the many religious
cavalcades held in Ethiopia, and are carried close to the priests
and crosses, sometimes directly overhead to give actual shade
and occasionally, it would seem, as processional items in their
own right. Frequently, beautifully-wrought silver crosses, or the
figures of saints, are used as finials; the green or red silk covers
are ornamented with silver and gold, and the fringes are hung
with silver bells.

The rulers of Morocco have also accorded great significance to
the umbrella, apparently out of respect for the people's belief
that sunshine is injurious to the holiness invested in sovereigns.
The royal model is extremely tall, perhaps 11 ft high, and flat-
topped. There are old accounts of it being carried by an officer
riding a mule alongside the sultan, who was likewise mounted—
a departure from the more common practice of having a bearer
running behind. On one occasion, centuries ago, a sudden gust
of wind broke the parasol as the royal retinue passed through the
palace gates, a mishap which greatly upset the sultan and was
generally interpreted as foreshadowing an early end to his reign.
For centuries the umbrella has been the distinguishing sign of the
sovereign in Morocco, and at one time its use was limited to him
and his immediate relatives, though the traveller, Ali Bey, once
boasted that he had had the honour bestowed upon him, possibly
because he had diplomatically presented the sultan with a particularly fine model.[1]

Many Europeans have seen in the royal palace the influence of the umbrella in the huge chandeliers which have the appearance of umbrella-canopies; and also in the royal camel howdahs, the roofs of which were once domed. When in the field, military officers of high rank had circular tents with tops of much the same shape, and with side pieces flowing down to the ground. An umbrella still forms part of the royal regalia, and Moroccans even today refer to the 'Shereefian Umbrella' rather than the throne as the principal symbol of kingship. When speaking of a wealthy man, a well-known expression is that 'the owner of an umbrella goes as it pleases him, in the sun or in the shade'.

Moroccan soldiers took a symbolic umbrella on their campaigns, using it as a rallying point and standard for their troops. When they were defeated by the French at Isly in 1844 they suffered not only the indignity of losing the umbrella but also of having the loss widely publicised in contemporary engravings, which show this particular model to have been surprisingly ornate and delicate. The modern royal umbrella is very tall, though rather more conical in shape than the majority of earlier models, which were either flat-topped or domed.

As in most other regions, the origin of the umbrella in Western Africa cannot be positively determined, though the article may have come from any one of several sources—perhaps being introduced by the Moslems who visited the area in the eighth century after Christ. Portuguese mariners reached the region in the latter part of the fifteenth century, and if they did not notice the royal umbrella there, they soon became aware of its importance when they reached the Indian Ocean. In 1498, Vasco da Gama sailed beyond the Cape of Good Hope and was received by the Sultan of Melendi (Malindi, near Zanzibar), who sat 'under a round sunshade of crimson satin attached to a pole' (the custom here having spread from the north, down the coast). Very soon the Portuguese were carrying umbrellas wherever they sailed, and so the West Africans would have been well aware of the umbrella by the early 1500s, if they had not already adopted it long before.

Also to be remembered is the legend that West Africa was colonised by Kisra, a Persian king who fled from Egypt to the Ethiopian city of Napata before moving west to found several separate states. Kisra has been tentatively identified with Khosrau II, the Sassanid king who conquered and ruled Egypt between 616 and 628, and is held responsible for a migration to West Africa, where he might have taken the custom of the royal umbrella. He is said to have founded the Yoruba states in Nigeria, where at one period the umbrella was the sole prerogative of the king. The Rev Samuel Johnson in his *History of the Yorubas* has this to say of the royal umbrellas:

> Those [umbrellas] of a chief are easily distinguished now by their size and quality. They are almost always of bright colours, usually of damasks. The size and number are in proportion to the rank of the chief, usually of European manufacture, though there is a distinct family of royal umbrella makers at Oyo who make those of the largest size. Most of the umbrellas, foreign or locally made, are decorated with certain emblems indicative of rank. About two dozen or more are used on these festive occasions.[2]

The umbrella has been, and often still is, extremely popular in most of the countries bounded by the Gulf of Guinea, especially in Dahomey and Ashanti, where few early visitors failed to comment on the custom. At the coronation of a king of Whidah (Ouidah, in Dahomey), in the 1720s, it was reported that:

> on the king's right hand stood a grandee with an Umbrello, which was only for show (the ceremony being performed at night). It was of the richest Cloth of Gold, the lining embroidered with gold, and the edge adorned with gold fringes and tassels. On the top was a cock of gilt wood, big as the life, and the pole that supports it six feet high and gilt. The officer who bore it turned it continually around, in order to cool the king.[3]

One European visitor to Dahomey, J. A. Skertchley, commented on the king's *agranhohwe*, or jaw-umbrella, which was thickly studded with eighty-four human jaw-bones and topped by a human skull. Each lappet of the umbrella bore six jaw-bones arranged like chevrons. This grisly object was proudly carried at the *So-sin* custom as a form of trophy. (Several local tribes were known to take jaw-bones from their dead victims, and sometimes those still living, though usually they contented themselves with up to four front teeth from the jaw of the latter.)[4]

Travelling in the Congo in the early eighteenth century; in this instance the parasol appears to have been for comfort rather than for honour

The famous traveller, Sir Richard Burton, has recorded some valuable impressions of the same country in the mid-nineteenth century; as soon as he landed in Dahomey he was approached by a 'Fetishman' protected by a white *kwe-hoor* tent-umbrella, somewhat tattered since 'these spiritual men care not to make a show of splendour.' Burton became very interested in the ceremonial usage of the many umbrellas; he recognised their symbolism as being similar to that of European heraldry and realised that, to the initiated, they gave some clue as to the station of the person they honoured. *Bosy-sau*, the bearer of the Royal Cane, was protected by two tent-umbrellas, one virgin white, the other decorated with emblems. Each chief was allowed an umbrella which was figuratively used to denote the chief himself, 'seven umbrellas have fallen' meaning seven chiefs had been killed. The *Gau*, or commander of the right wing of the army, had a model of red, blue and buff, whilst:

> the newly made Caboceer [chief] is presented with a virgin-white article of palace manufacture, and he is expected to illustrate it by his actions. The principal figures are knives and decapitated heads and faces, cut out of cloth and sewn on the alternate lappets of the valance.[5]

When Burton's party arrived at the royal capital, they were escorted towards the king's quarters, one part of which had a sort of verandah formed by four umbrellas:

> Those on the flanks were white, and mostly very ragged, sheltering the chieftainesses of the she-soldiers; in the centre, denoting the place where the king sat, they affected the gaudish tulip tints, dazzling hues, variegated, yet in perfect harmonies—scarlet, tender green, purple, white and light blue: an especial favourite was red and yellow. It is called in England Satan's livery, but when massed it excites the eye. These richly tinted umbrella-canopies are forbidden to all save royalty, and the king takes no little pride in them.[6]

The ruler of Dahomey was so anxious to acquire new models, as spectacular and gaudy as possible, that he once asked the British vice-consul, John Duncan, to order for him several of a specific pattern from London. Like most West African chieftains, he had an extensive collection of umbrellas, and during the *Sosin* custom he was sheltered by three wives holding:

Page 71 (left) His Highness the Yang di Pertuan Besar of Negri Sembilan, photographed in 1925; (right) King Daudi Chwa of the Baganda, photographed in the early twentieth century

Page 72 (*above*) Queen Mary and the Queen of Italy, escorted by Lady Guggisberg, walking under a state umbrella in the African village at the British Empire Exhibition, Wembley, 1924; (*below*) King Edward VIII, as Prince of Wales, receives a paramount chief during his visit to the Gold Coast, 1925

. . . gorgeous tent-umbrellas of cotton velvets, whilst a fourth protected him with a gay parasol. The first was a parody upon the *Sacré Coeur*—which the Dahomians admire, probably because it suggests tearing out the foeman's heart. Each lappet of the valance was alternately green and crimson; in the upper part was a large cross, red, or yellow, with a black or white border, and below it, of the same hue, an object manifestly intended for a human heart but broken into crockets. In the centre of this was a better-shaped heart with a small white medial cross; and both were disposed apex downwards. The second showed an upper line of white crosslets on black velvet; below it was a blue shark, edged white and yellow, with a red and purple eye, resting upon crimson or claret-coloured velvet, which was lined with a binding like that of the animal. The third, and the most splendid, was capped with a very heraldic wooden lion, painted the brightest saffron. The lappets showed the king of the beasts grasping in the dexter paw a white scimitar, and below it a biped, very Negro, with dazzling white knicker-bockers and no legs to speak of, vainly upholding a blue sword blade. Both figures were on red ground, *parsemé* with little white crosses. This umbrella was equally grandly lined, whereas the two former were white inside. The diameters varied from 6 to 10 ft, rendering them unmanageable in windy weather. The poles were 7 ft long, and instead of wires they had square rods connected by strings, probably brought by the Portuguese and easily to be distinguished from the rude native stick frames. They were kept open by a peg passed through the upper part of the handle.[7]

On subsequent occasions when the king received Burton, 'three royal umbrellas, blue, red and yellow, defended him from the sun, and he was fanned by three parasols'.[8] Burton and his party had their own umbrellas, which at first they had to close when appearing before the king, though later they were granted the privilege of keeping them open in his presence.

When the king prepared for war, he adopted dark-coloured umbrellas, his large honorific model being of the darkest indigo, whereas the smaller model he used for personal protection against the sun was chocolate brown. Whatever the size, it could have been no easy job to carry one of these umbrellas and the jaw-umbrella must have been particularly heavy with its grisly ornaments. A bearer no doubt enjoyed some small prestige—and perhaps shade—but his job was no sinecure. Several tribes in the Lower Niger, such as the Efik, Ibibio and Ibo, sacrificed holders of the office at the chief's funeral, together with the attendants connected with the royal sword and snuff-box. The objective of this well-known custom was to provide both material benefits and personal servants for the deceased in the next world.

Ordinary natives, such as those of the Ashira tribe, had to content themselves with arranging in advance to have an umbrella placed over their burial places. A century ago, many primitive models could be seen shading graves at Cape Coast Castle, in what is now South-West Ghana. This is reminiscent of the beliefs concerning shadows held by the Egyptians, and indeed there are other analogies between the customs of West Africans and those of the ancient Egyptians to suggest some old-established connection between the two, and to add credence to the legend of Kisra.

Just as an umbrella-shaped hieroglyph in ancient Egyptian texts signified the *khaibit*, or shadow, of a person so was the *sunsum* of the Akan of Ghana 'literally a kind of shadow . . . the mortal soul or consciousness of self . . . [with] the connotation of semen or begetting'.[9] So wrote E. L. R. Meyerowitz, who has equated the *sunsum* with the ceremonial fan, which the natives ally with the umbrella; when Gyasewaa, the queen mother (1656–79), demanded that the state umbrella be accorded her rank, she was only partially placated with a ceremonial fan. Gyasewaa was obviously envious of the *bidabiakyi*, the two-tier state umbrella of Akumfi Ameyaw II (1646–59), which his people termed *bitebiso*, translatable as 'someone sits on someone else'.[10]

Other tribes in and around the Gold Coast also attached great importance to the state umbrella; in the early nineteenth century T. Edward Bowdich, leader of a political-cum-exploratory force to the Ashanti—one of the Akan peoples—was received by a native monarch at Kumasi:

> At least a hundred large umbrellas, or canopies, which could shelter thirty persons, were sprung up and down by the bearers with brilliant effect, being made of scarlet, yellow, and the most shewy cloths and silks, and crowned on the top with crescents, pelicans, elephants, barrels, and arms and swords of gold; they were of various shapes, but mostly dome; and the valances (in some of which small looking-glasses were inserted) fantastically scalloped and fringed; from the fronts of some, the proboscis and small teeth of elephants projected, and a few

were roofed with leopards' skins, and crowned with various animals
naturally stuffed.[11]

When Bowdich arrived at the king's palace, he was greeted by:

> . . . counsellors, caboceers and captains . . . seated under their um-
> brellas, composed of scarlet and yellow cloth, silks, shawls, cottons, and
> every glaring variety, with carved and golden pelicans, panthers,
> baboons, barrels, crescents &c on the top; the shape generally a dome.[12]

These finials, termed *ntuatire*, are still retained today, each
having its own significance, symbolising the traditional power of
its owner, and often giving its name to the whole umbrella. Thus
Akomen (the horn of a deer or antelope) signifies the solidity of
the fighting power invested in a chief; *Tikorompa* (a symbol of
three heads) means that one head does not constitute a council;
and *Adowa a ogyina osono so* (an antelope standing on an elephant)
implies that great size does not alone entitle one to the lordship
of a state.[13]

Throughout the nineteenth century the British had a great deal
of trouble with the Ashanti, and often enlisted the help of enemies
of the Asanthene (the title of the king of the Ashanti). At the
battle of Dodowa in 1826, Atoko, king of Akwam, led the right
wing of an army under overall British command; at a strategic
moment in the battle he moved his large state umbrellas towards
the Ashanti force as if he were deserting to them, before suddenly
attacking and winning the day for the allied forces.

Later in the century, Britain had to launch another bitter
campaign against the Asanthene, King Koffee Kalcalli, and
when, on 4 February 1874, Sir Garnet Wolseley captured the
king's umbrella he had it sent to London to be presented to
Queen Victoria. It had forty-two ribs and measured 22 ft in
circumference. The cover was of alternate divisions of black and
dark crimson velvet, with a deep border of the same material
with gold trimmings; it was decorated with two lion's claws as
talismans, and with other good luck charms.[14]

In 1895–6 the Ashanti rebelled again, this time under King
Prempeh, and when the British forces finally subdued the up-
rising and dispatched Prempeh and his cohorts to the Seychelles,
the Asanthene's umbrella was once again presented to Queen
Victoria. During the early stages of the expedition, a newspaper

correspondent, clad only in pyjamas and armed with an umbrella, intervened in an argument between some of the Sierra Leone hammock men and the Wineba irregular troops. Umbrellas were useful additions to an officer's equipment on such campaigns, and feature in many sketches made during the expedition. The British soldiers were also much impressed by the native umbrellas, one officer comparing the long rows of enormous coloured umbrellas to the line of roundabouts at Barnet pleasure-fair!

Umbrellas were also used to shade other important articles of the royal regalia such as the Ashanti royal stool—a development of tree-worship—whose carrier was escorted by a flat-topped umbrella of *nsa* (camel's hair and wool), termed the *Katamanso*, or 'covering of the nation'. Similarly the regal gold-headed stick of the King of Juaban was sheltered by an immense, gorgeous umbrella of crimson silk. In 1876, the king was driven out of his land by the Asanthene, and appeared at Cape Colony with all his regalia. The stick was protected by its customary umbrella, borne by a panting attendant followed by three or four gigantic state umbrellas, each as large as a tent, topped with gilded figures which were the crests of war-captains. (The king himself was allowed a finial of gold as he was of the Asanthene's clan.)

Besides the *Katamanso* umbrella, the Ashanti have the ceremonial *bankyiniie*, with convex top, similar to European design, and the utility *akuromponkyiniwa* for everyday use. The people of Kumawu claim that the original *bankyiniie* covered copper statues of a mother and her three children, and originated from the Volta region. The Asanthene of today has about two dozen umbrellas, each of which is reserved for a special occasion; for instance, he sits under the *akokotan* (which has a top representing a hen with her chickens) when attempting to settle differences involving a chief. There was a time when he was not allowed to go outside, or to pass from one room to another, unless covered by an umbrella carried by one of the *kɔmekyimini*, or bearers, for the 'sky god must never behold the crown of the king's head'. When receiving an *Omanhene*, or paramount chief, the Asanthene would expect him to step from under his umbrella when greeting him, as a mark of respect.[15]

Many of the lesser West African chiefs still maintain their privilege of the umbrella, and some have even appeared at Buckingham Palace carrying their own elegant models of normal size but ornate design. Sometimes these have been specially made to order by London firms, but there are natives, notably among the Ashanti, who skilfully produce ceremonial umbrellas from various kinds of beautifully-coloured materials, including silk, felt, brocade and damask. They sometimes also make the utility *akuromponkyiniwa* from plain black linen, though these are often imported.

Some African tribes have used the umbrella for fertility rites and marriage ceremonies; the Bavili kept a girl approaching puberty in a secluded hut, and after ten weeks or so led her to her intended husband's dwelling under an umbrella. (The Ashanti still use the umbrella on such occasions.) Should this ritual not be observed, it was believed that the girl would be barren and the crops unsuccessful. A girl of the Tshi tribe announced her eligibility for marriage by being escorted in her best clothes under an umbrella, and the Baganda of Uganda considered it to be an essential feature of any wedding ceremony.

These various customs, several of which suggest Asiatic influences, are yet another part of the umbrella's story which cannot be fully explained, having gone unrecorded until their origins became lost in the distant past.

European travellers in Africa, no less than the Africans themselves, were addicted to the use of umbrellas, and in the nineteenth century the explorer Sir Samuel Barker was recommending to his compatriots:

> ... a couple of large carriage umbrellas with double-lining, with small rings fixed to the extremities of the ribs, and a spike similar to that of a fishing-rod to screw into the handle, will form an instantaneous shelter from sun or rain during a halt on the march, as a few strings from the rings will secure it from the wind, if pegged to the ground.[16]

Sir Harry H. Johnston also found the umbrella useful, and in his *British Central Africa* gave some hints on suitable outfits for travellers in the territory:

> Umbrellas: One black silk umbrella for the rain should be taken, but several good strong light sun umbrellas MUST be taken. These should

be double-lined, with a space between the linings—white outside and green within. They must be very LIGHT to hold. . . . Where the sun is felt even more than on the head is on the shoulders and along the spine. To shield the body from the sun, in fact, the only way is to carry a white umbrella, and this should be done on almost all occasions except when to do such a thing would be positively ridiculous, as, for instance, in the middle of a battle. There is no more effectual aid to the maintenance of health than to constantly carry a white umbrella when compelled to face the strong sunshine.[17]

Sound advice indeed, and no doubt explorers bearing umbrellas unwittingly impressed the natives because of the umbrella's symbolism of royalty. On the other hand, the flaunting of an umbrella on a chieftain's own territory might well have caused an awkward incident!

But though Europeans might escape to the sunnier climate of Africa, they could not escape European-style conventions and nowhere is the social status of the umbrella better reflected than in the *Praal and Pracht* (*sic*), or regulations for Cape Colony, dated 1752, which were issued by Ryk van Tulbagh, governor of an early Dutch colony in South Africa. These contain the following stipulations:

Article 6: It is ordered that no one less in rank than a junior merchant, or those among the citizens of equal rank, and the wives and daughters of those only who are, or have been, members of any Council, shall venture to use umbrellas.

Article 7: That those who are less in rank than merchants shall not enter the castle in fine weather with an open umbrella.[18]

But, status symbol though it obviously was to the Dutch in South Africa, the umbrella seems to have been largely ignored in the centre of the continent and on its southern tip. Several travellers noted its use without suggesting that the natives looked upon it as anything more than a knick-knack comparable with coloured beads and the top hat, those traditional attributes of African tribesmen. In 1875, Commander V. L. Cameron observed a native carrying an umbrella near Lake Tanganyika, and could see it only as a diversion:

I was greatly amused by one of the guides who displayed much pride at possessing an umbrella. He kept it open for the whole day, continually spinning it round and round in a most ludicrous fashion; and when we came to some jungle he added to the absurdity of his appearance by taking off his only article of clothing—his loin cloth— . . . the sight of a perfectly naked negro walking under an umbrella was too much for my gravity, and I fairly exploded with laugther.[19]

One suspects that many European travellers have overlooked the umbrella's symbolic importance to the natives; even an experienced boundary commissioner like R. A. Freeman could make the following, slightly ingenuous, remark:

I do not know why it is, but evidently to the African mind an umbrella is a special symbol of magnificence and dignity . . . even in so comparatively civilized a place as Sierra Leone the umbrella is the outward and visible sign of the dignity and importance of its possessor. In the latter town on any Sunday morning, native aristocrats, who on weekdays loaf about the streets and markets bareheaded, may be seen wending their way to church, their woolly pates surmounted by a shiny 'topper' and duly protected by a trade gingham.[20]

Even one veteran explorer, George Grenfell, shared his umbrella one rainy day with the *Kiamvo*, a ruler of the Southern Congo, simply out of politeness and diplomacy, without realising that the chief looked upon it as something more than protection, and that native rulers had been using it for centuries before it was well-known in Britain.

4 *The Middle Ages: the Umbrella in the Catholic Church*

Whilst the umbrella was very popular in Asia and Africa during the middle ages, its use in Europe was hardly extensive enough to constitute a fashion. There are few references to it as a costume accessory in the millennium following the sixth century, when, as mentioned in Chapter 1, a Roman lad died because he did not carry a parasol in hot weather. Those models that were available in Europe as dress accessories were expensive sunshades made by skilled craftsmen, probably almost exclusively in Italy. Waterproof umbrellas received scant approval, for their sturdy and durable construction meant that they were also heavy and cumbersome, disadvantages which were to hamper their popularity until about 1750.

Even so, there are one or two false leads from north-west Europe which have been interpreted as inferring that the costume umbrella was used in medieval Britain and France. Some old Anglo-Saxon dictionaries have given the meaning of *scur-scead* as umbrella, and refer the student to Caedmon's version of Genesis:

> *Nys unc wuht beforan*
> *To scur sceade.*[1]

Adam is complaining that when the hail showers come, he will have nothing to serve as a defence. As Caedmon was most probably unaware that any such thing as an umbrella existed, it seems more likely that the compilers of the dictionaries in question indulged in over-imaginative translation. A more realistic definition of *scur-scead* is 'protection against rain'.

In the thirteenth-century poem, *Blonde of Oxford*, the Earl of Gloucester's costly robe is soaked by rain and the hero, Jehan of Dammartin, remarks 'If I were a rich man, as you are, I would always carry a house within which I could take shelter; I should then not be soiled or be wet as you are'.[2] This curious phraseology has suggested an umbrella to some readers, though Jehan is actually taunting the wealthy earl, and causes some amusement among the latter's retainers who think they have a fool in their midst.

Nevertheless, it has been rumoured that the Normans had an umbrella—or perhaps a canopy—of twelve parts, which they might have introduced into England, possibly having learnt of it from the Norman colony which was established in Italy by the eleventh century. Certainly there is evidence enough to prove that the umbrella was known, if not widely used, on the Continent at this time, for it then formed part of the regalia of the Roman Catholic Church. Indeed, it is possible that laymen were reluctant to adopt it because of its importance in religious ceremonial.

The Pope especially favoured the umbrella, and seems to have adopted the idea of its ceremonial use from other rulers, conveniently overlooking its reputed connection with pagan gods. A possible clue as to the origin of the papal umbrella may lie in the twelfth-century mosaics in the chapel of St Sylvester at the church of the Santi Quatto Coronati at Rome. (See illustration, page 90.) These show the Emperor Constantine presenting royal insignia, including a brown and white striped umbrella, to Pope Sylvester I, who held office from AD 314 to 335. The mosaics represent the notorious Donation of Constantine, when the emperor supposedly handed over the primacy of the Church and the rule of the West to Sylvester in thanksgiving for his miraculous cure from leprosy: .

'We grant and yield up to our most blessed Pontiff Sylvester, universal Pope aforesaid, and to the Pontiffs his successors, our Imperial Lateran palace, and also the city of Rome, and all the provinces of all Italy and the regions of the West.'[3]

The Donation of Constantine is not now recognised as ever having taken place, and was probably the invention of some eighth-century prelate eager to justify papal claims to secular power in Italy. The mosaics in the chapel of St Sylvester serve, therefore, only to confirm what was already known from other sources, that the umbrella was used in Europe for symbolic purposes in the twelfth century. It is also apparent that the artist concerned was depicting contemporary styles rather than attempting accurately to represent the practice of Constantine's reign, for in one mosaic he shows a mitre in the shape of two triangles, which is a post-eleventh-century design.

Even so, it is quite possible that the emperor did include the umbrella in his regalia. Legend says that he received various insignia, including crown jewels and diadems, as symbols of his two-fold power as Caesar and high priest, from two angels. Perhaps an umbrella was among them, and if an angel with an umbrella sounds very much of a comic oddity just such a one is said to have been featured in an old book, *Curiosités Mystérieuses*, which has an illumination from a church in the city of Ratisbon (now better known as Regensburg). This angel is shown standing at the right hand of Jesus Christ and bearing a cross to which is attached a half-closed parasol. In the same city, the convent of Nieder Muenster formerly had a manuscript with a picture of the four evangelists which included umbrella-shaped trees, such as are occasionally found in Indian sculptures and drawings.

Descending to less exalted levels of speculation, Constantine could have adopted the umbrella from Eastern rulers. He was a great believer in Mithras the sun-god, and in the year 321 had ordered that the 'venerable day of the sun' be celebrated as one of rest. The previous year, his enthusiasm for Christianity had led him to forbid pagan symbols—save that of the sun—being represented on coins. We also know that one of his predecessors, Heliogabalus, was both a follower of the sun cult and a ruler who used the umbrella, so perhaps subsequent emperors had maintained the custom. This theory failing, Constantine could have adopted the umbrella on his own account when he transferred the capital of the Roman Empire to Byzantium (which became known as Constantinople, and is today Istanbul). This was a move that intensified Eastern influence on Europe.

Thus, notwithstanding the absence of any basis of fact behind the Donation legend, Constantine might well have included the umbrella in his regalia, and might later have presented it to Sylvester. Roman emperors certainly gave other customs to the Papacy, including the title of *Pontifex Maximus*. The title 'Pope' itself is of Eastern and African origin and was applied in early times to the bishops of the primatial sees of Carthage and Alexandria, in both of which the symbolism of the umbrella was well-known.

Authoritative opinion recognises that the papal umbrella had Eastern origins, though one may question the theory that these were specifically Mongolian. This would be too precise when one considers the importance of the umbrella throughout Asia.

> The symbol is very old. Its exact origin is not entirely clear but it is certain that it comes from the Orient, probably from Mongolia, where it was a sign of dignity and power, both human and divine. In Mongolia, only the highest military leaders were allowed to put up tents during campaigns. The big tents of the supreme commanders were shaped like *ombrellone*, Leaders of the Roman Empire adopted the symbol and at one time it was used to represent Papal authority in general.[4]

It has even been suggested that the religious parasol has some connection with the halo, and it certainly takes but a little imagination to identify the coronal symbol in early Christian art with a sunshade held directly behind the head:[5]

> its earliest and most usual form is that of a circle placed behind the head, which . . . is usually a solid plate of gold, sometimes filled with various ornaments or letters, and but rarely transparent; it also appears of various colours for different persons.[6]

Connecting the halo with the parasol is an intriguing concept, but it is more probable that the halo, symbolic of the sanctity of the person wearing it, represents the sun itself, and is not therefore identifiable, but only comparable with the parasol.

The Church having once adopted the umbrella, it soon became the custom for a high ecclesiastic to present an elaborate model to fellow dignitaries. Pope Paul I (AD 757–67) bestowed upon Pepin the Short a fine bejewelled umbrella after they had settled a dispute over possessions in North Germany. About AD 800, Bishop Alcuin of Tours sent to Bishop Arno of Salzburg a

Schutzdach, which in modern German means 'shed' or 'covering roof', 'to protect your venerable head from showers'; this was probably an umbrella.

The most conclusive evidence of the umbrella's importance in the middle ages has been found in the Utrecht Psalter, probably compiled in the ninth century, though other estimates of its date go as far back as the sixth. The Psalter shows David reaching out his hands towards a temple, whilst an angel stands behind holding a parasol above the king's head. The handle is slightly inclined and the finial rather large, but the cover, with its detailed ribs and tips, could be identical with modern design.

We know that the Egyptians and other nations had honorific umbrellas about the same time that David reigned (*circa* 1000 BC), and the famous biblical king must have been aware of the custom of shading royalty with a parasol. So it would not be surprising to find that he followed suit, even though there is no evidence in the scriptures to indicate that he did so. It is safe perhaps to assume that the artist concerned with this illustration was influenced by the customs of his own time, as was the case with the religious frescoes in Ethiopia.

The Utrecht Psalter was also the origin of the first representation of the umbrella in England, for in the late tenth century monks at Canterbury made a somewhat crude copy, with many little changes in the illustration of King David. His position remains the same, but the clothing has been changed to Anglo-Saxon styles, and the angel has become a decidedly humble servant. The umbrella, too, has altered, perhaps because the copyist was ignorant of the curious object, which was probably not then employed in English church ceremonial. Most fashion historians, ignorant of the origin of this illustration, have stated that it shows an Anglo-Saxon noble fitted out with the later costume accessories of his time, and have therefore concluded that the umbrella must have been used in England before the Conquest; whereas, in fact, this has never been substantiated.[7]

Another interesting medieval representation of the ecclesiastical umbrella is that on a jasper intaglio which shows a mounted bishop preceded by one servant bearing a cross, and followed by another holding an open umbrella with a thick handle and hemi-

(*left*) King David escorted by an angel with umbrella, from an original in the Utrecht Psalter. The umbrella was included to symbolise the king's royalty; (*right*) the first British illustration of an umbrella, copied from the Utrecht Psalter, *circa* AD 970

spherical cover topped by a large knob, its curious apple-like appearance being attributable to the rough workmanship on the original. The letters scattered around the design make up the name Janni N(omine) III, who was Bishop of Pavia from AD 884 to 924.

In 1177, Pope Alexander III awarded Sebastiano Ziani, Doge of Venice, the privilege of bearing the umbrella, in return for arranging a meeting between the Pope and Emperor Frederic of Germany, an occasion on which Ziani arranged for both his guests to be escorted by umbrellas. Girolamo Gambarota's picture in the Sala del Gran Consiglio, Venice, shows the Pope investing his host with the honour. The Venetians perpetuated the custom for many centuries, and several of Giovenni Canaletto's paintings of eighteenth-century Venice depict the Doge escorted by an umbrella-bearer. Of all ceremonial models, the Doge's was the most ornate, with extravagant decorations on the handle and cover. It survived the two other processional emblems of power in Venice, the throne and the sword, until 1797, when Napoleon took over the city.

By the thirteenth century, the more elaborate *baldachinum*—a four- or six-poled canopy—was beginning to take the place of the ecclesiastical umbrella, though it had already been occasionally

The Doge of Venice under his extremely ornate state umbrella used by the Church, and the ceremonial canopy held over a monarch dates back as far into history as the umbrella. The canopy and umbrella are, in fact, often identifiable with one another, notably in the Catholic Church and in wedding ceremonies. At Jewish weddings, a canopy known as the *huppah* was used to cover the bridal pair, *huppah* having formerly referred to the bridal chamber itself, of which the canopy was a symbolic representation. Originally a *baldachinum* of precious purple cloth adorned with golden jewels, it eventually became transformed into a loosely hung cloth on four poles. The custom has long since been discarded by many orthodox Jews. There are also countless representations and descriptions of canopies borne over monarchs—as in the British coronation ceremony when a canopy of cloth of gold is held over the sovereign—and this particular employment can be traced back to the old Egyptian concepts of the heavenly attributes of kingship being signified by a canopy or umbrella.

The earliest reference to a papal *baldachinum* has been found in the *Liber Pontificatis* (the relevant part of which was compiled between AD 496 and 530) which describes one given by Constantine to the Lateran basilica in the time of Sylvester I. Considering how little is known of Sylvester's reign it is a surprising coincidence that we can trace both umbrella and *baldachinum* back as far as this period and find that Constantine is reputed to have presented both to the Church.

  There is some confusion between the two objects in Latin (and other) descriptions of processions, and Charles de Linas has tried to differentiate between the various possible meanings of *umbella* and *umbracula* in most of the early accounts.[8] The umbrella proper is sometimes distinguished by the further name of *soliculum*, by which title the papal umbrellas are listed in an inventory of the time of Boniface VIII (1294-1303); these had silver fittings and white covers quartered with lions. A print in the Vatican Library shows a *soliculum* prominent at Boniface's coronation.

The four-poled *baldachinum* achieved its greatest popularity in the fourteenth century and more or less superseded the umbrella; the word itself derived from 'baldeck', a name given to a cloth of gold made at Babylon; is it only another coincidence that the period the Popes were absent from Rome (1309–77) is termed the Babylonian Captivity, and that the *baldachinum* became popular about this time? When Gregory XI returned to Rome from exile at Avignon, he was protected by a very elaborate model, the short sides of which were decorated with heraldic panels.

Despite the increasing use of the *baldachinum*, the umbrella still continued to play a part in papal ceremony. Ulrich von Reichental's *Concilium Constantiense*, produced in Augsburg in 1483, and telling of the Council of Constance, 1414–18, shows such a model, which was carried before the Pope on his journeys. The bearer was a man in armour, riding on a white charger covered with a red cloth sprinkled with gold. The massive cover was red and yellow, surmounted by a golden angel holding a golden cross. In the print, the umbrella looks as if it would envelop the horse should the rider accidentally let slip his burden, and both man and beast must have been exceptionally strong to bear their respective loads. Incidentally, this is the only picture to show the bearer as a knight of some standing; in others he appears to be of humble station. Furthermore, no other picture shows such a gigantic umbrella.

About this time, the umbrella came to be adopted as an heraldic device of the Papal States. Francesco Salviati's fresco in the Palazzo Farnese shows Eugenius IV (1431–47) commissioning Rannuccio Farnese as their military defender and the Pope is seated under the States' banner, on which an umbrella can be seen above the crossed keys. (See illustration, page 107.) The umbrella was then termed the *papilionus*, medieval Latin for a conical tent, and an inventory of the Vatican's treasures in 1435 lists a small *papilionus* of red and orange silk.

Soon, less illustrious people were adopting the papal device and the tomb of Raoul de Lannoy, erected in Folleville church, France, between 1513 and 1524, has something like an umbrella in the overhead stonework. From it are suspended draperies which open to reveal the tomb in a recess. The design is, significantly, North Italian, by Antonio della Porta. Much the same idea appears in Vincencio Carducho's *Dream of Pope Honorius* (painted about 1628), which shows the Pope under a *papilionus*

Page 89 (above) *The Battle of Umbrellas*, 1784; (below) *L'Averse*, by L. L. Boilly; one of many paintings featuring the umbrella or sunshade

Page 90 (*above*) Japanese women with parasols; (*below*) the Donation of Constantine; one of the twelfth-century frescoes in the Church of the Santi Quatto Coronati, Rome. Constantine the Great has just presented an umbrella, symbolic of sovereignty, to Pope Sylvester I

that is both lappetted and tasselled, with long flowing curtains falling to the floor. The Pope was still sometimes accompanied by a parasol, and occasionally this was to provide shade rather than to act as a symbol of honour, as in a cartoon by Francesco Ubaldini which shows Urban VIII (1623–44) examining plans for the rebuilding of Rome's walls. The day appears to be both sunny and warm, and the expression on the attendant's face is evident of his concentration on trying to keep the 7-ft sunshade—which is nothing like the usual ceremonial models—above the Pope's head. A later Pope, Clement XI (1700–21), is depicted in another Italian drawing described by Charles de Linas, being preceded by a servant bearing an open umbrella, while behind walks a colleague with a closed model which is identical to the first save for the point. Carried thus, the umbrellas symbolised a double honour paid to spiritual and temporal authority. When, later, this custom was dropped, parasols were replaced by hats of red velvet. M. de Linas stressed the artist's scrupulous accuracy and pointed out that the models depicted were similar to some of the later types used by the ancient Assyrians. He even suggested that the papal umbrella was a reproduction of these models, if not an original itself, a startling theory indeed.[9]

The true significance of the papal umbrella has now become more clearly defined, thanks largely to the researches of Monseigneur Barbier de Montault in the mid-nineteenth century, by which time the umbrella had almost disappeared from the papal regalia, due perhaps to its general popularity and its consequent incongruity as a ceremonial trapping. Mgr de Montault described the *pavillon* (the French term for the *papilionus*) as being cone-shaped—a semi-open umbrella almost—and surmounted by a sphere or cross; the material was striped with alternate bands in the papal colours of red and yellow. Once deemed the supreme insignia, it now exists only in the basilicas, where it is carried in procession or more often suspended from the wall.

The *pavillon* has a place of honour in the arms of the Papal States (two crossed keys, one of gold, the other of silver, tied to each other and surmounted by a *pavillon* lapped with gold and crimson). This symbol, entirely secular, is found wherever the Government has to

F

place its seal of administration: the apostolic Chamber [responsible for administration of Papal business], stamps, management of salt and tobacco, etc.[10]

The umbrella in this context has now been superseded by the mitre, but the head of the Chamber, called the Cardinal Cammerlengo or Cardinal Chamberlain, still retains a gold and crimson *pavillon* or *papilionus*, in his coat of arms, which can be seen on money coined, or buildings completed, during the *Sede*

Umbrellas of Pope Clement XI, 1700–21, carried in procession
to symbolise his spiritual and temporal powers

Vacante, the time when the Holy See is vacant. During this period, candidates for the papacy have been entitled to place the umbrella, together with the papal keys, on their arms. Hence the umbrella's significance in Italian heraldry: 'a sunshade of vermeil on a field argent, symbol of power, sovereign authority and true friendship.'

The *ombrellino* [or *umbella*], royal, princely and hierarchical symbol, is derived from the *pavillon*. This *ombrellino* . . . opens out like our parasols; it is red for the Pope, red or violet, according to the period, for the cardinals; green or violet for bishops; violet for certain privileged members of the priesthood, red and yellow for the Roman Senator, and with an embroidered crown for Roman princes.* An appendage—a sphere or a pennant—tops the article, which permanently rests in the ante-chamber, close to a cushion of the same colour. When the dignitary is in his carriage, the *ombrellino* is placed on the top; when he walks on foot, somebody carries his insignia before him.

In these two cases, the *ombrellino*, which is only used in certain exceptional circumstances, is covered with a sheath of the same colour. The cushion only appears outside when the dignitary entitled to it goes to a church or when it is necessary for him to kneel.[11]

Today these customs have all but died out, and many people entitled to ceremonial umbrellas are unaware of their privilege. The *umbella*, very much like the standard umbrella but usually flatter, is rarely seen, except in certain European villages, such as those around Arles in Provence, where in processions it is held over the parish priest, a custom descended by unbroken tradition from the last days of the Roman empire. A century ago in Britain, Catholic priests and bishops were sometimes escorted under an *umbella*, commonly of white or cloth of gold, but this has now been generally superseded by the canopy. It is the canopy, too, which is now most frequently used to cover the Sacrament in procession; only occasionally is the *umbella* substituted, so recalling the tradition of carrying the Sacrament close to the Pope on his journeys, and often under his honorific parasol.

* When a daughter of the Earl of Talbot died in 1840, an umbrella was carried behind her bier as she had been married to a prince of the Borghese family.

5 *The Utility Umbrella: 1500-1750*

IN THE EARLY sixteenth century the umbrella was known in many countries in southern Europe, mainly as a religious object but also as a fashionable novelty. Portuguese ladies, influenced, as we have seen, by their colonists' reports of the habit in Asia and Africa, had their servants carry shades over them, and it has been claimed that theirs was the first country to manufacture and introduce parasols into Europe. This can be discounted in view of the early Graeco-Roman and later Italian models but there can be little doubt that the umbrella was most popular in Portugal. The Spaniards, too, had noted the custom, being so close to Morocco, and those European countries near to Turkey were also aware of the oriental type of parasol carried in that country.

In the north, Dasypodius's *Dictionarium*, published in Strasbourg in 1537, lists *sonnenschirm*, or sunshade, though we do not know whether German people actually used it, or merely knew of its existence. It is thought that Catherine de Medici, daughter of the Duke of Medino, took a parasol with her to France in 1533 when she married the Duke of Orleans, later to become Henri II. Henri's mistress, Diane de Poitiers, must have coveted Catherine's fashions as well as her husband, for she possessed an extremely fine sunshade of an advanced but distinctly cumbersome design; fragments of the frame which have been preserved until modern times suggest it was of Chinese origin. Mary, Queen of Scots, in 1562 owned 'a little canopy of crimson satin of three quarters long, furnished with fringes and tassels made of gold and crimson silk, many little painted buttons, all serving to bear,

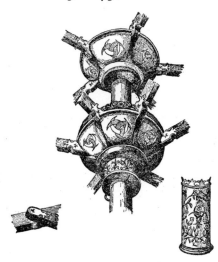

Part of the umbrella frame belonging to Diane de Poitiers
(mid-sixteenth century)

to make shadow for the Queen.' She would no doubt have acquired this during her stay at the French court a few years earlier.[1]

Several French authors have mentioned parasols being taken on hunting expeditions between 1550 and 1590, though Octave Uzanne felt such writers were 'having greater care of the splendour of the *mise-en-scène* than of absolute historical truth'.[2] The idea of a lady riding a horse across open countryside bearing a sunshade in one hand may be discounted, though it is quite probable that a servant might have carried a parasol to shade his mistress during pauses in the chase, just as had been done in the ancient civilisations. Furthermore the preliminaries to such occasions provided a good excuse to exhibit the latest fashions, and a few years later ladies would flourish the newest sunshade models from Italy as they assembled at the meet.

To the French in general, however, the parasol appears to have been virtually unknown in 1578, for in the *Dialogues* of Henri Estiennes, Celtophile askes Philansone:

> Have you seen a device which certain persons of rank in Spain and Italy carry, or have carried, less to protect themselves against flies than against the sun? It is supported upon a stick, and it is so con-

structed that it takes up little room when it is folded; but when it is
needed, it can be opened forthwith and spread out in a round that can
well cover three or four persons.

Philansone replies that he has never seen one, though he has
often heard about them, adding 'but if French women saw men
carrying them, they would consider them effeminate'.[3]

Two years later, Montaigne noticed that the ladies in the
Tuscan city of Lucca had sunshades which 'are used in Italy
since the time of the ancient Romans' but 'are rather a burden to
the arm than a protection to the head'.[4] A contemporary print
shows a nobleman on horseback carrying his ornate little parasol,
gripping its handle right at the end, which suggests that his
model was reasonably light.

Italian nobleman on horseback with a parasol, late
sixteenth century

As might be expected, accounts of specific sunshades at this
period continue to refer to those favoured by royalty. In 1582 a
sunshade valued at four ducats was included in the trousseau of
the Mantuan Princess Anna Catherine Gonzaga when she

married Archduke Ferdinand of the Tyrol. For many years the Hotel de Sully in Paris preserved a parasol called 'the *Pépin* of Henri IV' (1589–1610), whose large blue silk cover was decorated with golden *fleurs-de-lys*.* Very little is known of the manufacture of these umbrellas, for the trade has never been one to leave details of its craft for posterity. The utility models were mostly made by small firms who may have based their work on oriental practice, whilst the royal and ecclesiastical designs were the products of specialists, each stage of construction being entrusted to a different expert.

The first depiction of the umbrella in England, other than the drawing copied from the Utrecht Psalter, is in a painting of Sir Henry Unton—'one of the strangest and best-known pictures in the National Portrait Gallery'—showing the Elizabethan diplomat carrying a white umbrella against the heat as he rides from the Alps to Padua in the late 1570s. This particular scene is one of the many representations of episodes in Unton's career which border the main portrait. The artist is not known, and as the painting remained in private hands until 1884 it was overlooked by umbrella-historians before this date.[5]

In 1598, two years after Unton's death, Florio's *A Worlde of Wordes*, an Italian-English dictionary published in London, gave this definition: 'Ombrella, a fan, a canopie, also a testoon of cloth of state for a prince; also a kind of round fan or shadowing that they use to ride with in summer in Italy; a little shade.' Next year, John Minsheu's version of Percyvall's *A Dictionaire in Spanish and English* defined *tiresol* as meaning the same as *quitasol* (*quittar*, to ward off, *sol*, sun): 'a kind of hat used in China, very broad, which the principal men carry over their heads, with a short pole or staff, like a canopy, to keep off the . . . sun from them.' There are some fifteen recorded spellings of *quitasol* in English literature, the earliest being in a translation by Robert Parke, published in 1588: 'two quitasoles of silk.'[6]

English travellers used other very vague terms to describe the umbrella, including sombrero and shadow:

* *Pepin* is equivalent to the English word 'brolly' of much later date, an affectionate nickname for the article.

> They rowe too and fro and have all their marchandizes in their boates
> with a great Sombrero or shadow over their heads to keep the sunne
> from them, which is as broad as a great cart wheele made of the leaves
> of the Coco trees and fig trees, and is very light.[7]

Such amplification of the terms was seldom offered, and only those with experience of southern Europe or Asia would have understood the references. Nor could there have been many who appreciated the significance of the earliest noted contextual use of the word 'umbrella' in the English language, made by John Donne in 1609:

> We are so composed that if abundance or glory scorch and melt us, we
> have an earthly cave, our bodies, to go into by consideration and cool
> ourselves, and if we be frozen, and contracted with lower and dark
> fortunes, we have within us a torch, a soul, lighter and warmer than any
> without; we are therefore our own umbrellas and our own suns.[8]

Donne is thought to have travelled abroad in his youth and may well have seen umbrellas in use, or read of them in accounts of journeys in Italy.

W. Strachy made another reference in 1610, when describing the Bermudas: 'so broad are the leaves [of palms] as an Italian umbrello, a man well may defend his whole body under one of them, from the greatest storm rain that falls.'[9] When Ben Jonson mentioned a lady tripping up at the Spanish court, he wrote that 'There she lay flat-spread as an umbrella'.[10] But the most illuminating of these early writers is that famous pedestrian traveller, Tom Coryate, who in 1608 visited Cremona in Northern Italy, where he noted how sensible the umbrella was:

> Here will I mention a thing, that although perhaps it will seem but
> frivolous to divers readers that have already travelled in Italy, yet be-
> cause unto many that neither have been there, nor ever intend to go
> thither while they live, it will be a mere novelty, I will not let it pass
> unmentioned. Many of them [Italians] do carry other fine things that
> will cost at least a ducat, which they commonly call in the Italian
> tongue umbrellaes, that is, things which minister shadow unto them
> for shelter against the scorching heat of the sun. These are made of
> leather, something answerable to the form of a little canopy, and
> hooped in the inside with divers little wooden hoops that extend the
> umbrella in a pretty large compass. They are used especially by horse-
> men who carry them in their hands when they ride, fastening the end

of the handle upon one of their thighs, and they impart so large a shadow unto them, that it keepeth the heat of the sun from the upper parts of their bodies.[11]

Coryate does not seem to have brought a sample back with him to England, as did Robert Toft, who in his will, dated 30 March 1618, bequeathed 'an umbrello of perfumed leather with a gold fringe about it, which I brought out of Italy'. There must have been several other umbrellas in the country by then, brought back from abroad, and perhaps Richard Cocks returned home with his 'one faire kitesol [*quitasol*]' given him by a Chinese in 1615.[12]

Another traveller of the same period, Fynes Moryson, recorded an odd superstition which suggests that the recommended way to carry an umbrella was to tilt it behind one's head rather than hold it directly above:

> In hot regions, to avoid the beams of the sun, in some places (as in Italy) they carry umbrels, or things like a little canopy over their heads; but a learned physician told me that the use of them was dangerous because they gather the heat into a pyramidal point, and thence cast it down perpendicularly upon the head, except they know how to carry them for avoiding that danger.[13]

In 1624, Beaumont and Fletcher made a metaphorical allusion to the umbrella in *Rule a Wife and Have a Wife*, in which Altea says:

> Are you at ease now? Is your heart at rest,
> Now you have got a shadow, and umbrella,
> To keep the scorching world's opinion
> from your fair credit.[14]

Most of these early references suggest a sunshade, but in 1630 Michael Drayton inferred that the umbrella was being used in wet weather; it seems a curiously mundane object to introduce into the context:

> Of doves I have a dainty pair,
> Which, when you please to take the air,
> About your head shall gently hover,
> Your clear brow from the sun to cover;
> And with their nimble wings shall fan you,
> That neither cold nor heat shall tan you;
> And like umbrellas, with their feathers
> Shield you in all sorts of weathers.[15]

In Denmark at this time, the married gentlewomen 'wear upon their foreheads a French shade of velvet to defend them from the sun, which our gentlewomen [of England] of old borrowed from the French and called them Bonegraces, now altogether out of use with us'.[16] But what had we substituted instead—the sunshade? There is no evidence of this, and the rash of literary allusions in plays and poems is somewhat puzzling, for they are quite casual and give the impression that the umbrella/parasol were well-known, perhaps used, in England. Yet cognizance of either would surely have been limited to readers of Coryate and Moryson, (most other passing references, including many in *Purchas his Pilgrims*, being very vague) and those who had heard of it from travellers on the Continent.

The fashion had, however, certainly moved nearer home, for an engraving, obscurely assigned to the 'Collection of St Igny' and made in 1622, shows the 'French Nobility at Church' carrying sunshades; three years before, Louis XIII had 'five Turkish and German umbrellas for use in the sun'. And at this time the French comedian, Tabarin, was amusing people with his fantastically large felt hat, claimed as the forerunner of the parasol, though the comic can only be credited with popularising the new fashion.

During his stay in Italy, Van Dyck painted the Marchessa Elena Grimaldi carrying a parasol, *circa* 1627, but he seems to have found no excuse to include one in any of the paintings he made during his subsequent visits to England. In Holland at this time, several artists were including the parasol in their paintings. *Departure for the Hunt* by Philip Wouwerman, a specialist in scenes of the chase, shows a lady clutching a large-domed sunshade as she waits for the hunt to begin. Pieter Lastman, in 1619, had included a parasol, such as he might have seen during his Italian sojourn, in his *Nausicia and Odysseus*. Rembrandt's pen drawing, *The Adoration of the Magi*, includes a huge umbrella which has an oriental appearance, as does its bearer.

Another painter, Charles Lebrun, showed his patron, Pierre Séguier, Chancellor of France, with two parasols held over his head by pages. Traditionally this portrait is said to show Séguier entering Rouen on 2 January 1640, and if this is so the ambitious chancellor might well have been accused of trespassing on a custom which was then almost a prerogative of the blood royal.

Séguier's king, Louis XIII, had a wide range of models to choose from, having enlarged his collection of five in 1619; eighteen years later he owned eleven sunshades of taffeta and three umbrellas of oiled cloth trimmed with gold and silver lace. Handles of heavy oak and 32-in long ribs put the weight of some of these models up to 3½ lb. But at least people were now beginning to differentiate between models for fine and rainy weather. For the latter occasion there was a choice of oiled cloth, barracran or coloured grogram; oiled cloth was invented by one, Giacomo Marigi of Turin, whose family jealously guarded the secret for some years until it was discovered by other firms.

In October 1644, John Evelyn was able to buy an umbrella in Marseilles, and twenty years later, on 22 June 1664, he noted in his diary that he had seen the first Chinese paper umbrellas in Paris; they were sent to a Catholic priest called Tomson (*sic*) by the Jesuits of China. Evelyn described them as 'fans like those our ladies use, but much larger, and with long handles, curiously carved and filled with Chinese characters'. His *Kalendarium Hortense*, published the same year, has a title page which shows a black servant with a closed parasol.

When Maria Theresa was married to Louis XIV in 1660, she entered Paris by the gate of St Antoine, seated in her carriage and holding a small parasol over her head. At the ceremony itself, the mounted heralds-at-arms announced the order of events from the shelter of *des parasols coudés en biais*, slanted parasols, or perhaps awnings. Nicholas Bazin's portrait of the queen on horseback shows her sheltered by a parasol held by a page running behind her.

There are few literary allusions in French to the parasol for the remainder of the century, though actor Nicholas Barillon noted in 1676 that 'the days being very warm, the lady carried either a mask or a parasol of the most precious leather'. However, several contemporary prints show ladies carrying sunshades; in J. D. St Jean's *A Lady Walking in the Country*, the lady has her parasol in one hand and a walking stick in the other, manufacturers having yet to combine the two. The contemporary dictionaries

Lady Walking in the Country, by J. D. de Saint Jean,
after N. Bonnart

of Antoine Furetière and Pierre César Richelet both list *parasol*, and the latter mentions that it was carried only by women 'and then only in the spring, summer and autumn'.

*   *   *   *

In England, the umbrella was still untried, being considered strange enough to be classed under 'Utensils' in the list of exhibits at the extensive *Musaeum Tradescantianum*, or Collection of Rarities, assembled at South Lambeth by John Tradescant about 1656. Perhaps the Puritan régime discouraged the use of such a frivolous object as the gaily-coloured parasol and antici- pated the criticisms of a century later against the umbrella pre- venting the heaven-sent rain from wetting a person—the rain which falls upon the just and the unjust alike!

When Catherine of Braganza was married to Charles II in 1662, she is said to have brought an umbrella in her trousseau, which, if it followed the usual Portuguese design, would have been plain and large. Possibly Charles disliked the idea as much as he disapproved of other Portuguese fashions whose sombreness contrasted with the gay, daring clothes of the Restoration court. Sir William Davenant, in 1688, referred to the sunshade in *The Man's the Master*, set in Spain, in which the servant, Jodlet, tells Isabella she must think him a very desperate man 'for coming near so bright a sun as you are, without a parasol, umbrellia or a bongrace'.[17] There is said to be another allusion in one of John Dryden's plays, perhaps one of those set abroad, in which a character offers to carry an umbrella and fan for a noble lady.*

There is no evidence, however, to suggest that the parasol was in general use at Charles's court, though one or two historians tentatively assign its introduction to this period. When John Locke noted with approval the parasol being used near Mont- pelier in 1676, he inferred that it was but little known in his own country (and Locke had previously spent some years in London, where any foreign fashion would have first become popular): 'a

---

* An iron fireback, ascribed to the seventeenth century, now at Dyrham Park, near Chippenham, shows costumes of this period, and features a parasol. However, the fireback's country of origin is not definitely known, nor is its present owner prepared to vouch for its authenticity.

pretty sort of cover for women riding in the sun, made of straw,
something of the fashion of tin covers for dishes.'[18]

Certainly waterproof models were not yet being used in
London, and when it rained, pedestrians had to dash for shelter
or hide under cloaks. Samuel Pepys recorded in his diary for
6 April 1668: 'This day in the afternoon, stepping with the Duke
of York into St James' Park, it rained, and I was forced to lend
the Duke my cloak, which he wore throughout the park.' No
doubt the diarist was happier on another occasion when he
recorded offering his cloak to shelter four young ladies.

But some umbrellas, of a very different type, did appear at the
Court in 1682, as reported in *The London Gazette* in May of that
year:

> Windsor, May 16th; on Sunday after Morning Chapel, the ambassa-
> dor from the King of Bantam ... was conducted ... to his audience of
> their Majesties, in the King's presence-chamber, several of his retinue
> carrying launces, and two of them umbrellas, besides two of his
> master's servants, who also carried two umbrellas over his letter of
> credence and his presents, such as used to be carried by the same persons
> over the King himself (which they look upon as a great piece of state).
> Being come with the chief of his attendants into the presence, (the
> ordinary servants, with their launces, remaining in the guard-
> chamber, and they that carried the two great umbrellas having leave
> to come and stand within the presence-door) they made their obeisance
> as they approached his Majesty's throne ...[19]

In the evening, the ambassador presented the two great
umbrellas to Prince Rupert—and no doubt it was purely a
coincidence that with a few months the Prince was dead and the
Indonesian kingdom of Bantam in decline. For a long time
thereafter the King of Bantam's umbrella was almost a byword
in England, and even thirty-six years later *The Entertainer* sar-
castically mentioned that some of the then fashionable hats were
designed 'to score out a pattern of umbrellas for the King of
Bantam'.[20]

In 1687, British opinion of umbrellas in general was summed
up by the entry under 'Absurd Classifications' at a picture sale at
the Blue Coat Coffee House, St Swithin's Lane: 'a fine parcel
of Umbrellows with other curiositys.' The parcel may have been
a collection by an early enthusiast or an importer's accumulation

—perhaps even somebody selling off the umbrellas presented to Prince Rupert in the previous reign.

A contemporary definition confirms the impression that the umbrella was still considered unusual; Thomas Blount's *Glossographia*, 'an expounding of strange words', gives 'umbrello' as a 'fashion of round and broad fans, wherewith the Indians and from them our great ones preserve themselves from the heat of the sun or fire; hence any little shadow, fan or other thing, wherewith the women guard their faces from the sun'. This is similar to the definition for *l'ombrelle* given in Cotgrave's *Dictionary of the French and English Tongues* of the same period. The only practical use Englishmen had for the word as yet was a metaphorical one, and it thus featured in an epitaph on a church monument at Barnstaple in Devon, commemorating John Boyse, junior, who died on 1 May 1684 'in the sixth year of his age':

> Blest was the prophet in his heavenly shade
> But ah! how soon did his umbrella fade!
> Like our frail bodys, which, being born of clay,
> Spring in a night and wither in a day.

But some time in the period 1685–1705 the waterproof umbrella suddenly came into its own in this country. Unfortunately, no information has come to light which makes a more exact dating possible, but in 1696 Jonathan Swift wrote of Jack, who was representative of the Protestant Dissenters in *A Tale of a Tub*: 'A large skin of parchment . . . served him for a night-cap when he went to bed, and for an umbrella in rainy weather'.[21] Taken on its own, this passage does not prove anything, but when one considers that the umbrella definitely became popular around the turn of the century, this little-known reference, with an inflexion different to earlier allusions, could indicate the sudden popularity of the umbrella.

Yet if one accepts this, it really should be conceded that the passage suggests that men used the umbrella whereas all the evidence points to women as the only users of these new waterproof models, even though they were far more cumbersome than the dainty parasol and needed a much stronger grip. Kersey's *Dictionarium Anglo-Britannicum* of 1708 defines 'umbrella', or 'umbrello', more decisively than do previous word-books: 'a kind of broad fan or skreen, commonly us'd by women to shelter them from rain.'

Some fashion historians think the first umbrellas of convenience in England were used solely by upper-class women, as is suggested by a line in Thomas Baker's *The Fine Lady's Airs*, first played at Drury Lane in 1708; 'Mrs Trapes in Leadenhall Street is hauling away the umbrellas for the walking gentry.'[22] But a passage in Swift's *Description of a City Shower* shows that the umbrella was also carried by the working-class female— though the majority of people apparently still scurried for shelter in shops and doorways:

> Now in contiguous drops the flood comes down,
> Threat'ning with deluge this devoted town:
> To shops in crowds the dragged females fly,
> Pretend to cheapen goods, but nothing buy.
> The Templar spruce, while every spout's abroach,
> Stays till tis fair, yet seems to call a coach.
> The tuck'd up sempstress walks with hasty strides
> While streams run down her oil'd umbrella's sides.[23]

This, incidentally, is a passage much favoured by writers who, almost without exception, quote it as an early reference to the umbrella, and ignore, or are unaware of, the still earlier Swift passage from *A Tale of a Tub*, given above.

These first umbrellas were kept in coffee houses to shelter customers walking from the door to their carriages, but when a man borrowed one, even though conditions made it advisable, he was considered effeminate, as we see from a scathing advertisement in *The Female Tatler* for 12 December 1709:

> The young gentleman belonging to the custom house, that for fear
> of the rain borrowed the umbrella at Will's coffee house, in Cornhill,
> of the mistress, is hereby advertised that to be dry from the head to
> foot on the like occasion, he shall be welcome to the maid's pattens.

Best-known of all poetic references during this or any other period is that made by John Gay in 1712:

> Good housewives all the winter's rage despise
> Defended by the riding-hood's disguise,
> Or, underneath th'umbrella's oily shed

Page 107 (above) Eugenius IV commissions Rannuccio Farnese as defender of the Papal States, whose emblem is shown on the right-hand banner. From Francesco Salviati's fresco in the Palazzo Farnese; (*right*) Nigerian chieftain with honorific parasol, Lagos, 1956

Page 108 (*above*) the massive and ancient church umbrella at Cart-mel Priory, Lancashire; (*below*) Royal umbrellas in the London Museum belonging to King George IV (left), the Prince of Wales, and Queen Victoria (chain-mailed, centre)

> Safe thro' the wet on clinking pattens tread.
> Let Persian dames th'umbrella's ribs display,
> To guard their beauties from the sunny ray;
> Or sweating slaves support the shady load,
> When Eastern monarchs show their state abroad.
> Britain in winter only shows its aid
> To guard from chilly showers the walking maid.[24]

A later passage from the same poem tells us what men had to rely on when it rained: the surtout, a long, loose overcoat introduced about 1670. (Broad-brimmed hats were another popular aid to keeping off the rain.)

> By various names, in various counties known,
> Yet held in all the true surtout alone,
> Be thine of kersey firm, tho' small the cost,
> Then brave, unwet, the rain, unchill'd the frost.[25]

In 1717, St Nicholas's church, Newcastle upon Tyne, paid 25s for an umbrella, one of the earliest recorded entries for the article in churchwardens' accounts. This was then quite a reasonable price, though ten years later the churchwardens of St John Baptist's church at Chester paid only 10s for theirs. These early 'church umbrellas' were probably standard models, which were then very large, but not to be compared with some other really gigantic models that were later introduced specifically for churchyard use. One example at Bromley, in Kent, described in William Hone's *Table Book*:

> with its wooden handle, fixed into a movable shaft, shod with an iron point at the bottom, and stuck into the ground . . . stood seven feet high; the awning is of green oiled canvas . . . and stretched on ribs of cane. It opens to a diameter of five feet, and forms a decent and capacious covering for the minister whilst engaged in the burial service at the grave. It is in every respect a more fitting exhibition than the watch-box sort of vehicle devised for the same purpose, and in some churchyards trundled from grave to grave, wherein the minister and clerk stand.[26]

One famous example is still preserved at Cartmel Priory in Lancashire, but W. T. Hyatt's statement made in 1877 cannot be credited: 'Allow me to state that it is over 300 years old, and was used for carrying over the Holy Sacrament when borne to the sick.'[27] (See illustration opposite.)

G

In 1722, the city treasurer of Bristol bought an umbrella for 25s to protect the judges and magistrates as they walked from their carriages. In the same city the next year, the parish of St Philip's paid 5s for repairs to their umbrella. A decade later they gave 12s 6d for 'Five yards oil'd cloth for ye umbrella' and not till 1744 did they finally decide to buy a new model for £2 10s. By then prices had risen; on 11 November 1747, the parish of Priestley paid £3 0s 6d for its umbrella, a sum that included box and carriage. These old accounts suggest that umbrellas were only available from London, and perhaps one or two other large cities, whose traders imported them from the Continent.

*   *   *   *

Across the Channel, serious commercial production had started about the turn of the century, with some ingenious ideas being exploited by traders like Marius of Paris. His pocket parasol had folding ribs and a screwed, jointed stick in two or three sections, which was easily dismantled into a handy size for for the pocket. It could be hidden away until needed, when the snugly dry bearer could more easily tolerate the witticisms of his fellow pedestrians.

Part of an advertisement by Marius, a Parisian trader

Marius also made a collapsible square model that achieved little popularity though it was awarded a prize by the Académie Royale des Sciences, Paris. Another of his ideas was to produce a conventional model with a cord running from the middle of the stick to the ends of two of the ribs, to prevent the cover being blown inside out. Two disadvantages are at once apparent; the parts of the umbrella not thus secured would be just as vulnerable as before, and the user might almost strangle himself with the cords should the umbrella become unmanageable in a high wind! Nevertheless, Marius was a highly enterprising business man who publicised his products in poster-advertisements, some of which made the hardly credible claim that the weight of some models was a mere five or six ounces.

Other traders followed his example, and soon there were billboards in Paris publicising models which could be purchased from hawkers in the streets for fifteen to twenty-two francs. In 1734 the German newspaper *Frankfurter Intelligenzblatt* was advertising 'small umbrellas with fringes against the sun, and large yellow and brown ones for rainy weather'.

The sunshade had come into popular use in Germany in the 1720s, for *Frauenzimmerlexicon* of 1715 gives the following definition:

> Parasol really means a covering roof of oiled cloth supported upon a small pole, which females carry over their heads to protect themselves from the heat of the sun. In this country, however, females use it when it rains. It can be opened and shut.

Before the introduction of the waterproof umbrella, German women used great shawls called *Regenkappen*, but their tastes had been changed by French influences; though at first their menfolk were reluctant to follow this example. The umbrella no doubt took longer to gain acceptance in Prussia because of Frederick William's intense dislike of French ways. Even so, he allowed his son, the future Frederick the Great, and his daughter, to be escorted by a Moor holding a conical umbrella, and thus they were painted by Antoine Pesne in about 1715.

In Britain, also, the sunshade had crept into fashion more unobtrusively even than the umbrella, and had established itself by 1730 when a portrait was painted of the Duchess of Bedford showing her attended by a black servant holding a parasol in the Continental manner. The portrait, attributed to Charles Jervas, now hangs in Woburn Abbey. In this case the bearer was something of a status symbol, as even English ladies of rank generally carried their own sunshades.

The appeal of the parasol was twofold; it was not only becoming the fashion, but also provided a welcome substitute for the variety of inelegant veils and masks (and the daintier fans) which women had used for centuries to avoid sun-tan or freckles. For the time being, however, the styles available were stereotyped, often depending on what Continental exporters chose to send to England. If a lady wished for something original, she would have had to obtain it from Paris.

No Englishman is recorded as ever having been bold enough to follow the example set by some European gentlemen who carried sunshades for their own benefit. (Michael Morosini, a senator of high rank, is reputed to have been the first Venetian, the Doge apart, to carry a parasol, a small green model of delicate workmanship which he used as he was carried around the canals in his gondola about the middle of the century.) But then very few Englishmen at that time had even dared make a habit of using an umbrella in wet weather; Bailey's *Dictionarium Brittanicum* of 1736 confirms that this was a lady's privilege, for it defines 'umbella' as 'a little shadow; also an umbrella, a bongrace, a skreen which women wear over their heads to shadow them'.

But though it was gradually becoming more popular the parasol was still far from being a common sight in the mid-eighteenth century, and here one may conveniently leave it to peacefully develop into one of the most important of all fashion accessories, and concentrate on the more utilitarian umbrella, which was destined to suffer a storm of abuse before it became accepted as normal means of protection against the weather.

6 Popularity at Last for the Umbrella: 1750-1800

AFTER BEING AVAILABLE for half a century in Britain, the waterproof umbrella had still to achieve any real popularity as an article of everyday employment. Its occasional use was largely restricted to short walks between building and carriage, when it was held by a servant, or at a funeral, when it could be thrust into the ground. It was also carried by women if the day was really wet, but seldom merely in anticipation of a shower. For, once the novelty of owning an umbrella had worn off (along with its dubious waterproofing), it was apt to become more trouble than it was worth.

Even when an umbrella was new, its mechanics did little to encourage regular use. The heavy whalebone ribs were not hinged at the notch (the point where the ribs are secured to the stick), but strung on a piece of wire, an insecure arrangement that was constantly getting out of order. Furthermore, the ribs lost their elasticity if they became very wet, and then cracked if they were dried carelessly. The cotton cover, which seems unnecessarily large by modern standards, was claimed to have been rendered impervious to rain by oil or wax but, in fact, quickly became saturated and leaked. In any event, the entire contraption, mounted on its stout shaft, was far too heavy for convenient use, and when folded up it had to be carried under the arm, where, if damp, it would soil the clothing it was intended to protect. Just what had happened to the apparently far better models made by Marius is not known; perhaps his light designs had proved inefficient in practice, otherwise it is difficult to understand how the current technology could have produced such light and efficient frames as well as the clumsy articles just described. We do know, however, that by mid-century, Continental manufacturers were concentrating on eradicating these faults by improved methods of construction, with the result that the umbrella was then popular in France. Writing home to his father on 4 December 1752, from Paris, Lt-Col James Wolfe (later to win fame at Quebec) noted that:

> The people here use umbrellas in hot weather to defend them from the sun, and something of the same kind to secure them from the snow and rain. I wonder that a practice so useful is not introduced into England where there are such frequent showers, and especially in the country, where they can be expanded without any inconveniency.[1]

Yet the most famous pioneer of the umbrella in Britain—he is usually credited with its introduction into London, and even with its invention—did not obtain his inspiration from France. This was the philanthropist, Jonas Hanway, who, during his travels abroad, 'observed that the Persians are not cautious . . . of the sun in any degree equal to the Portuguese; for the last seldom travel without a cloak and umbrello'.[2] On his return to Britain, Hanway seldom ventured out without his new-found toy, and a portrait in his *Travels* shows him carrying a fine model. After his death in 1786, John Pugh wrote of him that:

> When it rained, a small parapluie defended his face and wig; thus he was always prepared to enter into any company without impropriety or the appearance of negligence. And he was the first man who ventured to walk the streets of London with an umbrella over his head; after carrying one near thirty years, he saw them come into general use.[3]

Despite this passage, it has never been clear whether Hanway used his umbrella for protection against the sun as well as the rain, for he was of delicate complexion and in ill health when he first started to carry it. Certainly he created a sensation when he first started walking the streets with his umbrella, and if he held it aloft on fine days as well as wet, we can better understand the mocking reception he received. Notwithstanding his important position in society as a founder of the Marine Society and a governor of the Foundling Hospital, he was fair game for the attentions of street urchins, who were encouraged, no doubt, by

Jonas Hanway, pioneer of the umbrella in Britain (as
imagined by a Victorian artist)

coachmen who saw their livelihood threatened by this new
method of shelter. Hanway was also criticised for defying the
heavenly purpose of rain, which obviously was to make people
wet, but he nevertheless persisted in carrying his umbrella, and
for some time all umbrellas were referred to as 'Hanways'.

Jonas Hanway's own model was preserved until the late nine-
teenth century, when it came into the possession of Mrs Elise A.
Strong, a descendant of the famous man. Later, in a letter to the
Secretary of the Marine Society, she wrote:

The umbrella, I deeply regret to say, I lost, but . . . the handle was ebony and all covered with small fruits and flowers. The outside was pale green silk and the inside lining was stone-coloured satin. When open, it was like a small tent, and when shut, it was all curiously jointed and would fold up to the length of a man's hand.[4]

Thus it would appear to have been of French manufacture, perhaps by one Reynard, who was producing 'parasols which fold upon themselves triangularly, and become no thicker or more voluminous than a crush-hat'. Such designs had a jointed stick and ribs that could be folded several times, and enjoyed some popularity.

In 1758 Dr John Shebbeare had the honour—though he would have been both unaware and unappreciative of it at the time—of publicising the advantages of an umbrella when he was sentenced to stand in the pillory for committing a libel. He borrowed a model, probably from some tea-room, and hired a servant to hold it over him to protect him from the rain, and perhaps the less gentle missiles of the crowd, on a cold December day. It appears that the Sheriff of Middlesex, Arthur Beardsmore, was favourably disposed towards the doctor, for he was afterwards put on trial for remitting part of the sentence without authorisation, and also criticised for permitting the umbrella.

In 1760, several umbrellas were shown in a print of Belvedere House included in a six-volume work called *London and its Environs Described*. Yet four years later a French visitor noted when touring the capital that 'it is a rule with the people of London not to use, or suffer foreigners to use, our umbrellas of taffeta or waxed silk', a further indication of the rude reception accorded to the bold bearers of such 'new fangled contraptions'.[5] There is even a suggestion here that umbrella-users may have suffered something harder than words from the street urchins. Horace Walpole gives us another viewpoint, recorded when he was staying in Paris the same year: 'What strikes me most . . . is the total difference between them and us [French and British] . . . they walk about the streets in the rain with umbrellas to avoid putting on their hats'.[6]

One very old umbrella, perhaps British made, with a tab reading 'No 1, England, 1765, Kendall' has been preserved by

Kendall & Sons of Leicester. It has a brown wooden stick 3 ft long and 2 in in circumference, with a slightly thicker flattened handle. The whalebone ribs are 26 in long, with metal stretchers. The fabric—of later date—is of green silk with a faded yellow border. This would seem to be a very early model made in Britain, for in 1766 a Mr Heath had to send to Genoa for a

Early umbrellas in England; one impression of the
cumbersome models available in the late eighteenth century

supply of umbrellas, for which he was continually receiving commissions. His sister wrote from Exeter on 2 November that 'we find our umbrellas very useful. They are coming in fashion here; several people have got them; they do very well in a still shower; but we cannot manage them in windy weather'.[7]

The Marquis of Caraccioli made the following comments on Paris fashion in 1768, and one may safely assume that much the same applied as the umbrella was adopted in London—though rainy days surely must have been more frequent than once a month:

> For some time now, it has been the custom never to go out without an umbrella and to submit to the inconvenience of carrying it under the arm every day for six months in order to use it, at a generous computation, possibly six times. Those, however, who do not wish to be taken as belonging to the vulgar herd, prefer to risk a wetting rather than be looked upon as pedestrians in the street, for an umbrella is a sure sign that one possesses no carriage.[8]

In the following year, a company obtained the exclusive privilege of hiring out parasols to pedestrians inconvenienced by the sun as they crossed the Pont Neuf, in Paris. Customers could take a parasol from an office at one end of the bridge and return it to one on the other side. It was also planned to extend the field of operations to other public places in the French capital. This particular scheme eventually came to nothing, though when H. W. Bunbury engraved his *View of the Pont Neuf at Paris* in 1771, he unflatteringly depicted a man of menial appearance using a cheap-looking parasol.[9] Variations on the idea of hiring out umbrellas were introduced from time to time, but never lasted for very long.

In 1769 the following entries were made in the church-wardens' accounts at Ulverston:

	£	s.	d.
June 3rd 1769: to John Cannon for a pike for ye umbrella			8
7th 1769: W. Kendal for a Churchyard umbrella		2	2	0
Carriage of do. from London		3	11
A Canvas cover		1	0

W. Kendal might have had some connection with the Kendall responsible for the umbrella described on page 117, and could have been the importer or agent in this case; churchyard umbrellas were still apparently only available in the capital 280

miles away. The iron pike supplied by John Cannon was attached
to the stick and thrust into the ground to save the clerk having
to hold it over the minister as he read the burial service. These
church umbrellas were sturdy affairs; the Reverend James
Woodforde had one held over him during a funeral service one
January, when it withstood the most unfriendly elements. 'The
wind blowed very strong, and snow falling all the time, and the
wind almost directly in my face that it almost stopped my
breath.'10

A rival fashion appeared in the early 1770s and was said to
have been the brainwave of the Duchess of Bedford. This was
the calash, a collapsible hood of black silk, mounted on four or
five semi-circular ribs of whalebone or cane—hence the name,
which had hitherto applied to a carriage with a similarly constructed hood. The miniature version gave protection from the
sun, and on a windy day had the advantage of being more snug
and less unwieldy than the umbrella—unless the wearer was
going directly into the breeze, when the calash was liable to act
as a wind trap.

                    *   *   *   *

Meanwhile, in America, the popularity of the umbrella was
rapidly increasing, though the emphasis there was more on sunshades, a distinct improvement upon the giant fans, some 18 in
across, which colonial women had been using to protect themselves from the sun. In 1738, Quaker Edward Shippen had a 9s
umbrella imported into Philadelphia aboard the *Constantine*,
and, two years later, a belle in Windsor, Connecticut, who
carried an umbrella imported from the West Indies, was mockingly emulated by her neighbours, who balanced sieves on broom
handles! But by 1762 models were being advertised in Boston
newspapers, and in June 1768 the following advertisement
appeared in the *Boston Evening Post*:

> Umbrilloes made and sold by Isaac Greenwood, Turner, in his
> shop in Front Street, at the following Prices: Neat mahogany frames
> tipt with Ivory or brass ferrils, 42s 6d plain; others at 40s; printed at
> 36s; neat Persian Umbrellas compleat at 6 10s and in proportion for
> better silk. Those ladies whose Ingenuity, Leisure and Economy

leads them to make their own, may have them cut out by buying Umbrella sticks or Forms of him; and those Ladies that are better employed may have them made at 15s a piece.

Oliver Greenleaf had advertised 'very neat Green and Blue umbrellas' in the same paper the previous month, and another Boston trader stocked 'unmade setts of Sticks for Umbrilloes for those who wish to cover them themselves'.

In 1772, a Baltimore shopkeeper imported a parasol from India which caused much local comment, by no means all favourable. Philadelphia swells and doctors tried to encourage the fashion by claiming it would keep off fever and sore eyes, while other people condemned the practice as a ridiculous effeminacy. Quaker Nathaniel Newlin carried an umbrella to the Chester meeting, but other Friends remonstrated against this evidence of wordly spirit, even though Newlin had sat six times in the Pennsylvania Assembly. And one Quaker girl who flaunted an umbrella was reproached thus by a senior member of her community: 'Miriam, would thee want that held over thee when thee was a-dying?'[11]

Old Indian records dated 1786 mention that 'the Cheyennes killed Shadows—father winter'. Though this seems rather vague for a definite interpretation, an authority on Indians, E. S. Curtis, has stated that it 'intimates that Shadow was the first Dakota to use an umbrella'.[12]

*   *   *   *

Why the Baltimore shopkeeper mentioned earlier had to send halfway across the world to India for an umbrella is difficult to understand. He could surely have obtained one more easily from Boston, or from the West Indies, for quite a few native-made models were finding their way from the Caribbean to the American mainland, and even to Europe. In 1776 a Mr Stockdale bought one in Granada and used it at Cartmel, in Lancashire. Six years later, another Stockdale spent 15s on a silk umbrella from Paris, a good bargain this, unless the entry in the family accounts refers to some form of carriage charges.[13]

This silk model would have been made by *les boursiers*, the manufacturers of gloves, purses and girdles, who had been united into one community in August 1776. An edict of this date announced:

> They alone also still have the right to make and manufacture all sorts of umbrellas and parasols in whalebone and in copper, folding and non-folding, to garnish them atop with stuffs of silk and linen, to make umbrellas of oil cloth, and parasols adorned and ornamented in all sorts of fashion.[14]

Such manufacturers at first produced the entire umbrella, though later they made only the frame, which was then passed on to a milliner who would cover it to the customer's specification. Because fashions were constantly changing, only a small stock of completed sunshades was available in the French capital. A typical umbrella would have as a stick a metal tube containing a spiral spring which acted upon and pressed upwards an inner rod.

> To this inner rod were jointed the stretchers, which in this construction were placed above the ribs instead of below, as in the ordinary form; besides which they were much shorter so as to admit of their being concealed by the covering. By the elasticity of the spiral spring contained in the hollow stem, the inner rod was pressed outwards and lifted the stretchers, and by their means raised the ribs also, so that in its ordinary or natural state the umbrella was always open, and would continue so unless constrained to remain closed by a catch. On releasing the catch it consequently sprang open. In order that it might be easily closed, four cords were attached to four of the ribs and passed to the handle; and a loop embracing these cords passed down by the side of the handle, and enabled the possessor to close his umbrella without difficulty.[15]

The main characteristic of most designs was greater compactness, as the makers of the late eighteenth century continued to concentrate on reducing the cumbersome size of their products. They fitted detachable handles instead of the heavy, ringed copper balls, by which umbrellas had been previously carried, and hinged the 30-in ribs at the notch instead of stringing them on to a wire. About 1785, Gosselin of Amiens invented the *parasol à ressort* which had for the stick four steel tubes which could be telescoped into each other; we have, of course, seen that the Chinese had thought of the same idea 3,000 years earlier (see page 32). Gosselin is also said to have been the first to use

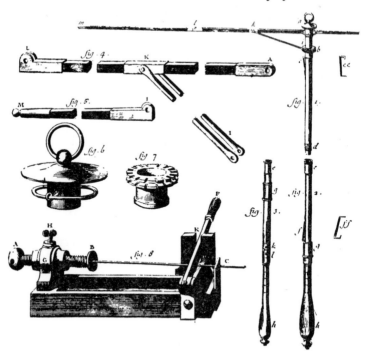

Umbrella frame and rib-cutter, France, *c* 1760

hinged ribs of pliable steel, which could be folded to two-thirds of their length. Other models had a spring fixture for opening and closing. It had also been the custom to stretch one round piece of material—calico or silk—over the frame; now it was thought better to draw out the sections with chalk, and cut out each individually.

In England, such few manufacturers as there may have been were barely established and certainly of very modest output. A Bristol shopkeeper was advertising in a local newspaper on 19 August 1775 that he had 'a stock of silk and other umbrellas', which were probably imports. These included some red models which were not well received—hardly surprising since almost anybody carrying an umbrella in Bristol was still liable to be hooted at! An exception was the Reverend Henry Shute, rector of nearby Stapleton, who had been provided with one back in 1766, and because of his clerical garb was able to carry it around unmolested. Incidentally, his parish's generosity in providing this protection may be compared with its yearly allowance of £2 towards his accommodation. Clergymen were, in fact, among the first to buy umbrellas, perhaps because they had some experience of churchyard models, and their cloth guaranteed immunity from offensive criticism. This increasing interest and slight rise in demand seem to have been reflected in a decrease in prices, for whereas on 20 May 1777, an umbrella for the vestry at Sculcoates, Hull, cost 23s, another purchased at Cranbrooke six years later cost only 12s.

About this time, Mr Warry of Sawbridgeworth, in Hertfordshire, ran from the church porch one wet Sunday to fetch an umbrella to shelter his family on the way home—greatly, it was said, to the envy of his neighbours. In Stamford, a Mr Renouard pioneered the fashion when he imported a model of Chinese origin from Holland; another man who introduced it to one Midland town was thereafter known as 'Umbrella' Harvey. There is also a story, probably apocryphal, about a brother-in-law of the first Sir Robert Peel who, whilst on a packet-boat, noticed a fellow-passenger holding a green umbrella: 'You have a musical instrument there, sir,' he said. 'Might we ask you to favour us with a tune?' Whereupon the passenger proudly opened out his umbrella and explained its purpose.[16]

Also in the 1770s, there appeared in London the notorious Theodora de Verdion, of whom it was said, 'in her exterior she was extremely grotesque, from her large cocked hat and bagged hair, with her boots, cane and umbrella, which she carried in all weathers. The latter of which she invariably carried in her hand, resting upon her back'.[17] De Verdion's mannish appearance caused some doubt as to her true sex, so that she could not have been exactly helpful in promoting the right sort of 'public image' of umbrella-bearers.

In August 1777, the *Westminster Magazine* sought to enlighten its readers with a description of 'a silk umbrella, or what the French call a Parisol. It is fastened in the middle of a long, jappanned walking cane with an ivory crook head. It opens by a spring, and is pushed towards the head of the cane when expanded for use'. The writer obviously felt that very few people

could have had the opportunity to examine the models which
were by then being imported into the country.

A London footman, John MacDonald, proved just as vulnerable a target for the taunts of passers-by as had Jonas Hanway,
when he started carrying his silk umbrella in the streets of the
capital in January 1778:

> If it rained, I wore my fine silk umbrella; then the people would
> call after me: 'What, Frenchman, why do you not get a coach?' In
> particular, the hackney coachmen and chairmen would call after me,
> but I, knowing the men well, went straight on and took no notice. At this
> time there were no umbrellas worn in London, except in noblemen's
> and gentlemen's houses, when there was a large one hung in the hall to
> hold over a lady or gentleman if it rained, between the door and their
> carriage. I was going to dine in Norfolk Street, one Sunday. It rained;
> my sister had hold of my arm; and I had the umbrella over our heads.
> In Tavistock Street we met so many young men, calling after us:
> 'Frenchmen! Take care of your umbrella.' 'Frenchman, why do you
> not get a coach, Monsieur?' My sister was so much ashamed that she
> quitted my arm and ran on before, but I still took no notice but
> answered in French or Spanish that I did not understand what they
> said. I went on so for three months, till they took no further notice of
> me, only 'How do you do, Frenchman?' After this the foreigners,
> seeing me with my umbrella, one after another used theirs—then the
> English. Now [1790] it is become a great trade in London and a very
> useful branch of business. When I went to a public-house, where
> servants meet in the evenings, I was called by the name of Beau
> MacDonald, or the Scotch Frenchman.[18]

MacDonald's assertion that umbrellas were not then worn in
London contradicts the information we have about the fashion
in the period prior to 1778 (when Hanway was still alive), and
one can only assume either that he let his pioneering pride waive
strict accuracy, or that the new vogue was in danger of lapsing
into oblivion.

Whether James Watt, the famous engineer, was unaware of the
umbrella or merely scornful of it we do not know, but when, on
16 October 1779, he wrote to his partner, Matthew Bolton, asking
him to come to Cornwall to help with the pumping engines at the
mines there, he added: 'Bring with you a waxed linen cloak, and
one for me, as it rains here every day—there is no going out even
for a few miles without being wet to the skin.' Or perhaps it was

Page 125 (above) Parasols, 1880–90; (below) Umbrella Cottage, Lyme Regis, Dorset; an early example of the nineteenth-century enthusiasm for the umbrella

Page 126   (*above*) the all-important parasol at Ascot, 1908; (*below*) at Henley, 1926

just that he knew too well the kind of reception they would have been given by the turbulent Cornishmen.

English Quakers, like their American counterparts, were also showing some opposition to the new fashion, and at one of their yearly meetings in London issued a warning against 'the wearing of those new-fashioned things called umbrellas'. Yet one Friend in Ireland, Benjamin Clarke Fisher, liked the new idea so much that he ordered a model from London, and actually rowed down the river Shannon to meet the ship bringing it in. Whether this was to try it out as soon as possible or to acquire it secretly, we are not told, but what use would an umbrella be if it was not intended for public display? Yet eventually the Quakers came to favour the umbrella, and it even became symbolic of their meekness.[19]

Ownership of the first umbrella in Scotland has been attributed to Dr Spens of Edinburgh in 1779, though other accounts put forward Alexander Wood as the pioneer three years later. Wood's popularity was enormous, and would have protected him from any initial public reaction just as well as his large gingham saved him from the rain. Dr John Jamieson imported a yellow umbrella, with waxed cloth covering the rattan ribs, into Glasgow from Paris in 1782–3 and much enjoyed relating how, when he commenced unfurling it in the streets, crowds of people followed him in amazement.

Conspicuous and often derided though these pioneer umbrella-carriers may have been, however, they did at least escape the kind of penalty incurred by James Heatherington who introduced the top hat to London streets on 5 January 1797. Women fainted and boys screamed, and Heatherington ended up before the Lord Mayor, by whom he was bound over to keep the peace in consideration of a sum of £50, 'having appeared on a public highway wearing upon his head a tall structure having a shining lustre and calculated to frighten timid people'.

Enthusiasm for umbrellas was now increasing, and the fact that they were also becoming the subject of anecdote and carica-ture indicates that though the fad was now established it was still uncommon enough to be commented upon.

One such anecdote which appeared in the *Glasgow Constitu-tional* about this time, tells how:

H

When umbrellas marched first into this quarter [Blairgowrie, near Perth], they were sported only by the minister and the laird, and looked upon by the common class of people as perfect phenomena. One day, Daniel M—— went to pay his rent to Colonel McPherson, at Blairgowrie House; when about to return, it came on a shower, and the colonel politely offered him the loan of an umbrella, which was politely and proudly accepted, and Daniel, with his head two or three inches higher than usual, marched off. Not long after he had left, however, to the colonel's surprise, again he sees Daniel posting towards him with all possible haste, still o'ertopped by his cotton canopy . . . which he held out, saluting him with 'Hae, hae, Kornel, this'll never do, there's no a door in my house that'll tak' it in; my verra barn-door winna' tak' it in.'[20]

About 1780 'B.E.' sketched *A Mushroom Frogstool and Puff* which satirised broad-brimmed hats and the umbrella. In January 1782, James Gilray drew *A Meeting of Umbrellas* showing a soldier, a citizen and a fop adopting the mode and apparently getting tangled up. (See opposite.) Two years later, a drawing entitled *The Battle of Umbrellas* was published, depicting a crowd of people near Westminster Abbey also getting into difficulties as they struggled to raise their umbrellas during a sudden shower. (See illustration, page 89.)[21]

Yet there was still apparently some resentment at the use of the umbrella by certain sections of the community and those of the 'underprivileged' who adopted the new mode invited sarcasm, if no worse. William Cowper, in his *Task*, published in 1784, commented thus on the country girl dressing above herself:

> Expect her soon with footboy at her heels,
> No longer blushing for her awkward load,
> Her train and umbrella all her care.[22]

The following year *The Town and Country Magazine* remarked that 'the philosophers of puppyism may be met with in every part of the town, constantly with umbrellas under their arms'. Even in France there were those who considered the fashion an attribute of *la gent français trottemenu*, of the 'mice', the French breed of imitators, and who dubbed anyone carrying an umbrella as *une veritable petite-maîtresse*, or dandy. This is not so surprising when we hear that in 1786, men in Lyons were carrying parasols of red and white material trimmed with blonde lace.

A Meeting of Umbrellas, by James Gilray, 1782 (people
obviously found these new gimmicks hard to handle)

Robert Louis Stevenson, however, had his own theories as to
the types of people who would have adopted the new fashion.

> Consider, for a moment, when umbrellas were first introduced into
> this country, what manner of men could use them, and what class would
> adhere to the useless but ornamental cane. The first, without doubt,
> would be the hypochrondiacal, out of solicitude for their health, or the
> frugal, out of care for their raiment; the second, it is equally plain,
> would include the fop, the fool and the Bobadil. Any one acquainted

with the growth of Society, and knowing out of what small seeds of
cause are produced great revolutions, and wholly new conditions of
intercourse, sees from this simple thought how the carriage of an
umbrella came to indicate frugality, judicious regard for bodily
welfare, and scorn for mere outward adornment, and in one word, all
those homely and solid virtues implied in the term RESPECTABILITY.[23]

Thus in 1787 the *Philosophical Transactions* of the Royal
Society gave the following approbation; 'if the weather be rainy,
an insulated umbrella may be carried in one hand'. Such distinguished encouragement gave the English manufacture of
umbrellas new impetus, and some of the early models had acorns
attached to the handles, the superstitious believing that as the
oak was sacred to the god of thunder this would prevent their
being struck by lightning. This particular fear was by no means
new as, at least a decade earlier, the 'Lightning Umbrella' had
been invented by one, Dubourg, who adapted Benjamin Frank-
lin's theories on lightning conductors to his design.

In 1787, Thomas Folgham, of Cheapside, was offering for sale
'a great assortment of his much approved pocket and portable
umbrellas, which for lightness, elegance and strength far exceed
anything of the kind ever imported or manufactured in this
Kingdom. All kinds of common umbrellas prepared in a particular way that will never stick together.'

These pocket models sound most attractive, and one wonders
why they enjoyed so little popularity, unless, perhaps, they
proved impracticable in use.

Another type of 'pocketable umbrella' was brought over to
England by a French priest, a fugitive from the Revolution. It
was described in *Notes and Queries* as being:

> . . . lightly constructed, with steel and brass ribs, which bent back in
> the middle, like the handle of a parasol. It was covered outside with
> bluish-green silk, and lined inside with yellow. The handle was of
> mahogany—and made to bend back with two joints. The whole when
> expanded formed a light but very serviceable umbrella of the usual
> size; but the same, when folded up in its case, could easily be carried in
> a coat pocket.[24]

Though the *canne à la parapluie* was being marketed in France,
the walking-stick umbrella was not yet common in England, and
models were generally carried under the arm or slung across the

back. Ferrules had rings attached through which ribbons could be threaded. Men's designs had Siberian bones and tusks polished and etched for handles, whilst Continental manufacturers hollowed out grips for ladies so that small writing sets, perfume flasks and powder-puffs might be carried; other types had lorgnettes, telescopes and stilettoes fitted. Small quantities of oiled silk were available for the better covers, and the fan parasol was introduced, with the stick hinged to the frame so that the cover could be tilted to shield the face; this was destined to become the most popular of all vogues.

The last decade of the century did much to dispel the somewhat effeminate image that the umbrella had once had, and when the gentlemen of the Third Estate were excluded from the Paris Assembly on Louis XVI's orders on 23 June 1789, they proudly sheltered from the pouring rain under their umbrellas. At the other end of the social scale, the umbrella was also adopted at the time of the Revolution by the fishwomen, *Les Poissardes des Halles*, who found them doubly useful as protection from the rain and a claim to equality with ladies of the nobility. They also served a further purpose, for when Théroigne de Méricourt, the 'Amazon of Liberty', fell foul of the *Poissardes* on 31 May 1793, they dealt her a torrent of blows with their umbrellas, inflicting injuries which later led to her insanity. Poetic justice, perhaps, for she was alleged to have sworn to make herself a parasol out of the intestines of Queen Marie Antoinette!

On the other side of the Channel, another type of radical was finding an umbrella useful. John Thelwall, shortly after his release from prison, addressed a meeting on 25 October 1795 to protest against the high price of bread, and a contemporary caricature shows him addressing a mob while a gleeful rogue holds an umbrella over him. Soon the umbrella had become part of the standard equipment of any orator.[25]

As a contrast, the year before, George Stubbs had executed an elegant pottery plaque for Josiah Wedgwood, showing a young lady in a carriage holding up a parasol. With this ultimate seal of approval, the umbrella can truly be said to have earned acceptance from all classes of society.

      *   *   *   *

A hazard inseparable from the carrying of an umbrella has always been its awkwardness on a windy day, and this a certain group of people in the 1770s seriously sought to turn to good account; the aeronauts of the age were eager to exploit the potential suggested by the spectacular antics of umbrellas and their owners during a gale.

Perhaps their ideas were stimulated by Japanese paintings of women jumping from the Kiyomizu temple with umbrellas to gain favourable answers to their prayers. Or by the Chinese *Shih Chi*, completed in 90 BC, which tells of Ku-Sou wishing to kill his son, the Emperor Shun, by inveigling him to a tower to which he then set fire. Shun tied together a number of conical umbrella hats and jumped to safety.

In the 1680s, much the same idea had occurred to a Siamese monk, who amused the royal court by his daring descents aided by two umbrellas fastened to his belt. L. Sebastian Lenormand read of this and made a few practice trials, holding in each hand an umbrella which had cords from the tips of the ribs to the stick, to save the covers turning inside out. He recommended the idea to Joseph Montgolfier, who in 1779 made a sort of parasol $7\frac{1}{2}$ ft in diameter. It was attached to a basket carrying a sheep and, pushed off a high tower, the basket was floated safely to the ground.

Two years later Jean-Pierre Blanchard's design for one of the many theoretical French flying-machines included an open umbrella above the craft for use when an emergency necessitated abandoning the craft. He tested the idea by dropping a small dog attached to a specially constructed umbrella 23 ft in diameter. Restiff de la Bretonne's romance, *La Découverte Australe*, written at this time, also refers to an umbrella designed to serve as a parachute on an 'air-machine'.

Thomas Martyn had the same idea, 'an umbrella to afford an easy descent should the balloon burst', and included it in his *Hints on Aerostatic Globes* in October 1784. Blanchard believed that Martyn had appropriated his brainwave for a 'fall-breaker' but was magnanimous in his protests. 'As to its being adapted to Air Balloons, let the discovery be yours: experience has convinced me that it can answer no manner of purpose.' Martyn retaliated with the observation that the air resistance of an umbrella was obvious to anybody who had ever used one in a gale.

The French general, Beurnouville, put theory into practice in 1793 when he attempted to escape from his Austrian prison at Olmutz, using an ordinary umbrella. Unfortunately, his 40-ft descent proved faster than he had anticipated and he was lucky to break only a leg.

A little later, Robert Cocking noticed an umbrella falling from a balcony with the handle downwards, but turning over before reaching the ground. He exploited the idea with 'inverted-cone' model parachutes in 1835, but met his death two years later when his personal experiments with a full-sized model ended with a drop of several thousand feet from a balloon.

In 1838, John Hampton built a parachute in the shape of a 15-ft wide umbrella. It had thick whalebone ribs 8 ft long, supported by bamboo struts, and a 'handle' of copper tubing 11 ft long. At Cheltenham, Hampton attached his apparatus to a balloon which rose to a height of 9,000 ft, when he cut it loose, allowing himself and his umbrella-parachute to fall free. After a descent which took thirteen minutes, the aeronaut reached the ground safely, having completed the first of the seven successful falls he was destined to make.[26]

Not only did the umbrella play its part in the development of aeronautics but in 1844 it was also used in testing the prototype of the inflatable rubber life-raft. Lieutenant Halkett designed a boat consisting of a canvas outer cover and an inflatable inner tube—and powered by an umbrella and a paddle! Similarly, when, in 1875, Captain Boyton was demonstrating his Boyton Life Dress for use at sea, he used an umbrella as a sail for part of his journey down the Thames from Westminster to Greenwich. Then, in 1896, somebody else invented the 'Umbrella rig' for sailing boats: 'the sail when spread had precisely the appearance of a large open umbrella, the mast of the boat forming the stick. Twice as much canvas could thus be carried as by any other form of rig, and the sail had no tendency to heel the boat over'.[27]

7 The Fashionable Parasol and Umbrella

By 1800, JUST as the parasol and umbrella had achieved separate identities after centuries of being confused with each other, so their fortunes had also now become disassociated; the parasol was firmly established as a luxury item of fashion, but the vicissitudes of the umbrella were far from being over. True, it was popular enough at the turn of the century to be suggested as a taxable item on which money could be raised for the French wars (William Pitt commented, 'Tax umbrellas, and make the Bishops order the prayer for rain to be read in all the churches till the end of the month!'); but there were still many who doubted its usefulness. When Eton schoolboys began to carry umbrellas, headmaster John Keate protested that the 'effeminate innovation' was making the college degenerate into a girls' school. Whereupon some boys took a notice-board inscribed 'Seminary for Young Ladies' from an establishment in Slough and fixed it above the entrance to Upper School!*

Novelist Captain Marryat sketched *The Umbrella* and added the comment that 'They make these here things sadly too small for good-sized people'.[1] Others could fault the umbrella because 'it is now made of such materials that it is in the hands of every class' and 'it is within these twenty years become so common that no servant runs a message without one'. The umbrella, in

---

* It took a master of a much later generation to show an enviable faith in the protection of an umbrella. Two boys, for some reason or other, were heaving a 16-lb. weight on to the arch into Weston's Yard when the Provost appeared. Warned of the overhead danger, he promptly put up his umbrella and passed nonchalantly underneath.

fact, had become more an article of utility than an item of fashion. Most models were still hopelessly inelegant, and only the very few made to measure by certain traders were considered suitable for people of refinement.

A fashionable alternative introduced about this time were umbrella bonnets, broad-brimmed hats which at one time threatened to displace the lady's umbrella. William Heath satirically depicted these bonnets as capable of covering the wearer and her two male escorts, and in the middle of his engraving drew a skinny, ragged umbrella-seller bearing a placard inscribed 'Pity the Poor Starving Umbrella'.[2]

The parasol, on the other hand, was light and elegant, constantly changing in style and available in a variety of materials and colours. Serving both as a dress accessory and a shade from the sun, it could also be used to hide the modest bearer from unwelcome glances, or, gracefully handled, could prove a most effective aid to coquetry. Commented *The Lewes & Brighthelmston Journal* in 1823: 'It is the custom now not to hold up the parasol, for it only prevents the men getting a glimpse at us, but merely to carry it dangling in the hand to show that you've got one.' To enable the parasol to be dangled in this ostentatious manner, manufacturers shaped the ivory handles to end in rings. Fashions in general, however, were still being influenced by the modes in Paris where, in 1821, a most elegant parasol was made of:

> India muslin embroidered with a beautiful border in feather stitch instead of fringe, the edge is finished with broad Mechlin lace, about four inches in breadth; the parasol is lined with azure blue, shot with white, the stick and handle are of polished steel, the thick part is beautifully wrought, and the handle is formed like the leaf of the acanthus.[3]

Just how numerous and varied in design and material had parasols now become is evident from this passage from Octave Uzanne's book on the sunshade:

> We can follow in the innumerable *Monitors* of elegance which appeared from 1815 to 1830, from year to year, from season to season, the variations introduced into the decoration of the little ladies' parasols. Look for a moment: here are sunshades, covered with coloured crêpe, or damasked satin, with chequered silk, streaked, striped or figured; others enriched with blonde or lace, embroidered with glass

trinkets, or garnished with maribou feathers, with gold and silver lace, or silk trimming; the fashionable shade is then very light or very deep, without intermediate tones: white, straw-yellow, pink or myrtle green, chestnut and black, purple-red or indigo. But a hundred pages would not suffice us to catalogue these fashions of the sunshade.[4]

Contemporary parasol modes catered mostly for women, the designers naturally concentrating on a market in which fashions could be relied upon to change profitably each season. The umbrella, on the other hand, had become stereotyped, save for occasional improvements in its mechanics, and only a few men bothered to order special models, like one in an 1830 style which was covered with myrtle-green *gros de Naples* without a border, fitted with a handle of Chinese laurel and surmounted by a simple plate of gold.

That leader of society, Beau Brummel, developed his own peculiar taste in umbrellas after his disagreement with George IV; during his exile at Caen he affected an unusual model, its ivory handle being decorated with an unflattering portrait of the king complete with well-curled wig. The cover was of silk and, when furled up, it was protected by a snug case of the same material.

George IV's own umbrella was of pinkish silk with a striped border; the frame was of metal, the ribs and stretchers of solid stout wire, and the handle stubby, wooden and brass-ended. (See illustration, page 108.) Several other European monarchs were also now carrying umbrellas, not as emblems of their royalty but for protection from rain, and in doing so came in for much adverse comment. One of the first to suffer was Frederick III of Denmark (1648–70) whose huge and heavy cotton model was held to be undignified and far removed from the elegant designs of his French counterpart, Louis XIV.

Louis Philippe of France was strongly criticised for adopting a somewhat untidy-looking umbrella, which his subjects maliciously suggested he had acquired during a visit to England. The caricaturists of the period delighted to portray it as characteristic of the avarice of 'M Prudhomme', as they termed the king. Under such influences the umbrella rapidly came to signify austere and citizenlike behaviour, symbolising the 'domestic virtues of order and economy' if not narrow-mindedness and mediocrity. And not only in France, as witness this opinion expressed by a Scottish writer:

> A daft like walking-stick indeed is an umbrella! Gie me a gude blackthorn, wi' a spike in't. As for carrying an umbrella neath my oxter [armpit]—I hae a' my life preferred the airm o' a bit lassie cleekin mine —and whenever the day comes that I'm seen unfurlin an umbrella, as I'm walking or sitting by mysel', may that day be my last, for it'll be a proof that the pith's a' out o' me.[5]

Typical gentleman's umbrella of the 1840s, bulbous and clumsy; it was not uncommon for umbrellas to be carried over the shoulder

But it was in France that the deterioration in the umbrella's once proud status was most evident for, to quote Uzanne again:

> Anglomania had not yet penetrated, as in the present day [1883], into French manners; and the dandyism of 1830, which pretended that the carrying of a walking-stick required a particular skill, repelled the umbrella as contrary to veritable elegance. The umbrella was countrified, the property of gaffer and gammer; it was tolerable only in the hands of anyone who had long renounced all pretensions to any charm and dreamed no more of setting off in the promenade the haughty

profile of a conqueror. In the cross-ways, in every public place in Paris, the large parasol, red, or the colour of wine-lees, had become, as it were, the ensign of the strolling singer who retailed Béranger to the crowd; it served as a shelter for acrobats in the open air; it surmounted the improvised trestles of the sellers of tripoli, an universal ointment; it ascended even the chariot of the quacks; later on it served as a set-off for the plumed helmet of Mangin, the pencil merchant; and it is still under a copper parasol . . . that the one-man orchestra causes an excitement in the court-yards by ringing his little bells.[6]

Small wonder, then, that it became the custom to denigrate the umbrella as 'a bastard born of the walking-stick and the cabriolet'. This remark, attributed to Honoré de Balzac, contrasts with that of the French dandy, the Count d'Orsay, who declared a few years later that, failing a good carriage, he would have a good umbrella.

In 1841 the scorn and sarcasm finally culminated in the publication of the anonymous *Physiologie du Parapluie par deux cochers de fiacre*, which contained many allusions to Louis Philippe, who was represented as a bazaar merchant who attained the Chinese throne and royal umbrella. The book contained some vestiges of umbrella history, and suggested, tongue in cheek, that Pythagoras had introduced the idea into Greece; its most useful contribution was to demand the abolition of cloakroom fees for umbrellas left in public buildings. The rest of the contents are superficial, though allusions to contemporary political and social conditions are of interest.

As the umbrella steadily descended the social scale, so the more elegant sunshade continued to increase in popularity as a fashionable accessory of dress. In 1834 Verdier, a leading vendor in the Rue Richelieu, was selling stock models in unbleached silk casing, mounted on a stick of American bindweed ornamented with gold and carved coral. Magazines and newspapers of the time, both in English and French, constantly refer to the multitude of models available.

Ladies found that the carriage ride was the best occasion on which to flaunt the latest line in parasols and thought the 'marquise', or fan parasol, 'perfectly calculated for that purpose'. The 'marquise', also termed the 'coquette' as it was so suitable for flirting, was said to have been invented by the Marquise de

Pompadour. It had been introduced into England fifty years before and had enjoyed intermittent popularity ever since. The bearer did not have to tilt the parasol to shade herself from the sun, but had merely to adjust the cover by the hinge; this was judged 'peculiarly convenient for the carriage'. In 1839, *poul de soie chinée* trimmed with fringes and an embroidered border was popular as a covering for the 'marquise', while parasols, in general, if intended for carriage use, had to be as ornate as possible. For the lady who drove her own horse and trap there was a somewhat unwieldy model with a whip at the end, as well as large carriage umbrellas which could be attached to the vehicle itself.

In 1844, William Sangster patented the 'Sylphide' parasol which had a spring at the end of the handle so that the shade could be closed with the hand that was holding it; the shaft was metal, the ribs of whalebone, and the handle and point of carved ivory, the covers usually being made of taffeta fringed with lace in the French fashion. But colours had become so sombre that 'A Country Girl' in 1848 was moved to exclaim 'Shame on us if another summer sees the brown parasol' when she wrote to *The Art Union* to suggest 'something more in harmony with blue skies and bright flowers'. She herself suggested designs based on the lilybell (with exterior stick), on the geranium leaf, and on butterfly's wings! Her ideas for 'these pretty anti-Apollos', though novel and ingenious, were never adopted, although one firm subsequently produced the cycloidal shape which dispensed with a full-length central pillar.[7]

Parasols did, however, tend to show greater frivolity at the halfway point of the century, and often the fringe and cover were chosen to match the bearer's gown; the great point was to have a stick 'as long and as elegant as a sunbeam'. Should a lady have recently suffered a bereavement, *The Book of Etiquette* permitted her to recover from her loss with the aid of a fancy-coloured parasol, black shades to complement mourning dress not being introduced until some years later.

When a lady was on foot, she preferred a larger-sized parasol with a stronger stick, or even, perhaps, a walking-stick umbrella. In one or two umbrellas, covers, ribs and all, folded away inside the stick to form a 'rhabdoskidophoros or walking-cane umbrella', just one of the many gimmicks that came on the market at various times. Others included handles that contained perfume or writing materials, a rack-and-pinion device to open out frames, a curtained cover, a stick fitted with a dagger, and many more novelties besides, some distinctly reminiscent of ideas which had been developed on the Continent some time before.

One could also have a flask fitted to the handle of one's umbrella to catch drips from the cover; though quite why anyone should have wanted to collect rainwater is hard to see, unless it was intended for the benefit of travellers abroad who wanted to be sure of at least an occasional drink of pure water! The lopsided umbrella, and another with a cranked handle, had the same purpose in mind—and suffered the same disadvantage. They were designed to bring the cover directly over the head of the bearer, but the idea did not work out in practice as the umbrellas proved highly unstable. Later on, the Germans produced a similar design, with one side of the umbrella elongated to cover a lady's bustle. Other bright ideas included umbrellas with windows, another which whistled when erected, and one which had sponges sewn to each rib-tip![8]

One Victorian writer, in *The Gentleman's Magazine*, had this to say of the owners of such novelties:

> Yet the proprietors of such fanciful gewgaws as folding umbrellas, umbrella walking-sticks, pocket umbrellas and the like are few and far between. They are either inventors seeking gratuitous advertisement for the offspring of their brains, or creatures who, without their wits, and with a superfluity of vanity, angle for a cheap notoriety in the exhibitions of an eccentric appendage.[9]

Gimmicks became less frequent in the second half of the century, when the straightforward umbrella came back into favour on both sides of the Channel. The common gamp still remained an abomination in the eyes of the fastidious, but superior models, slimmer and lighter as the result of further improvements in manufacture, were now available at a price. Parasolmakers had temporarily run out of new ideas and were content to ornament old favourites with somewhat fantastic trimmings. About 1855, sunshades *à la Pompadour* were very popular, though, in fact, they differed little from the 'marquise' type with hinged stick. Sticks on all models were usually of carved mother-of-pearl, ivory or rhinoceros horn, the covers being made from satin bordered with trimmings, or decorated with gold and silk.

About this period, the parasol was adopted by the Empress Eugenie, wife of Napoleon III, as a symbol of her unquestioned leadership in the world of fashion. Fifteen years later, she still retained it during her exile in Kent, where a visitor remarked that she then favoured a sun-umbrella of buff-colour lined with green silk, whilst many of her suite were using parasols as walking-sticks. Such seemingly trivial observations obviously fascinated Victorian newspaper readers, who once had been delighted to learn that their queen and her consort, having been caught in the rain at East Cowes, had been lent an umbrella by an old postman, who received a five-pound note for his courtesy. Doubtless people would have been equally intrigued to learn that the queen's bill for parasols in 1870 amounted to £52 9s.

Fashions then, as now, were easily swayed by what royalty were favouring. In 1867 Alexandra, Princess of Wales, had adopted a very heavy parasol to support her as she walked, a rheumatic illness having left her with a slight limp. Not only was her parasol adopted but her limp also! There is no record, however, of anyone following the example of Queen Victoria when she had chain-mail interlining concealed in some of her sunshades after someone had tried to shoot her.

Such cumbrous shades as these did not, as it happened, clash with the current trend as, from the early 'sixties, designs had taken on a heavier look due to thicker handles and more solid ferules. 'Parasols are generally worn of a plain shape without any trimming and are rather large . . . to serve as an umbrella as well as a parasol' commented the *Englishwoman's Domestic Magazine* in 1861. Some of the once popular pagoda shapes still persisted, usually with large unfringed coverings, though a few were edged with lace. These pagoda parasols had the ribs converging lower down on the stick than was usual, then suddenly bending up so that the centre of the cover was peaked. But within five years the pagoda design was out of favour, and smaller parasols with long ivory or ebony handles and striped covers of brocaded silk started to appear. Other fashions of the decade were the domed

THE UMBRELLA QUESTION;
Or what it would have come to, if Some People had had their way.

The Umbrella Question; a *Punch* cartoon, 1862

shape, bright colours, and china knobs on the tops of the sticks; the silk mixture known as Gloria was also introduced as a covering.

From the early 'seventies onwards, the mode and covering of sunshades varied with every season. By 1883, Uzanne could report that:

> . . . they have become artistic in all points, and after having been in turns in spotted foulard, and set off with ribbons and lace, as with the parasol walking stick, the maroon or cardinal-red parasol, have succeeded the checkered taffetas, the Madras cretonnes, the Pompadour satins, the figured silks. Their handles are adorned with porcelain of Dresden, of Sèvres, or of Longwy, with various precious stones, and with jewels of all sorts; and lately, among some wedding presents, amidst a dozen sunshades, one remarkable specimen was entirely covered with point lace, on a pink ground clouded with white gauze, having a jade handle with incrustations of precious stones up to its extreme point. A golden ring, gemmed with emeralds and brilliants, attached to a gold chain, served as a clasp for this inestimable jewel.[10]

Page 143 (*left*) Typical umbrella-seller in the nineteenth century; (*right*) Neville Chamberlain with the notorious umbrella he took to Munich

Page 144 (left) Ascot, 1968 —one of the few occasions when the parasol is still carried in this country; *(right)* the umbrella in modern fashion, from a 1968 rainwear collection. It is styles like this that might re-establish the umbrella

In Britain, some double-armed models were produced, with the stick forking just above the handle to frame the face. This was thought to make an enchanting picture of the bearer, even though it rather hampered her in twirling it elegantly, or coquettishly toying with it. A much more successful innovation, which was extremely popular everywhere for a decade or so, was the Japanese paper parasol with a bamboo handle, as used by Sarah Bernhardt when she appeared in *La Dame aux Camélias* in Paris in 1881. In 1886 fashions, notably in Britain, became very elaborate again; ribbons and ribbon-bows reappeared near the point and handles, while the sunshades themselves were 'little more than daintily puffed veils at the end of sticks'. Soon, carved animals and insects featured on the handle; sticks were as long as alpenstocks and knobs as large as billiard balls. The *en-tout-cas*, a waterproof parasol (introduced much earlier as a *paratout*), also enjoyed wide popularity and was available in a variety of colours and with all sorts of handles.

Towards the end of the century, covers of chiffon and fancy silk on very long sticks came into vogue. Ladies carried their parasols closed, while gentlemen had their own 'city umbrella', a tightly-rolled and immaculate silk-clad stick which served as sceptre to the bowler hat's crown. As such it settled down to a long period of popularity, even if it was more often carried neatly furled than ever actually used for protection. But at least it was a great improvement upon the untidy gamp of earlier years and marked the final acceptance of the umbrella by well-dressed men.

*   *   *   *

The first twenty years of the new century in many ways reflected the parasol styles and public attitudes of the old; even murmurs of unseemly behaviour were revived when Edward VII went for a ride on a tricyle bearing an umbrella—the *lise majesté* here, perhaps, reflecting less upon the king himself than upon the umbrella's Edwardian image, as 'the Englishman's sceptre of empire by which he ruled!'. Fashions changed as frequently as in mid-Victorian times, every year seeing a different mode; only two things remained unaltered, the 42-in length of the sticks and the dictum that colours should harmonise with the

I

costume of the bearer. In 1900, covers were of lace lined with chiffon, whilst the handles were china knobs; then Chantilly lace, flowered silk and enamelled handles came into favour. The year 1903 saw the brief reign of Pompadour silk, the next year it was chiffon's turn again, spread on to massive frames which suddenly disappeared in favour of smaller sizes.

Early in Edward VII's reign, a French newspaper, *Le Gaulois*, noted that Londoners were using red umbrellas striped with yellow 'to the great joy of negroes living in the English capital, who were reminded of their native land by these multi-coloured gamps'. But this was a short-lived fad, superseded by another in 1904, when an unknown English inventor produced a transparent umbrella, the 'secret' covering material of which was not so clear as glass, though the bearer could, it was said, at least recognise his friends through it. '*Le parapluie vitré? C'est une conception, mon Dieu!*' commented *Le Soleil*, which imaginatively attributed its invention to a Russian prince anxious to keep a ready eye out for mad dogs!

In the second decade, the outbreak of war caused a lull in the changing vogues, most noticeably on the Continent, where the parasol temporarily disappeared towards the end of the war. At home, the previous year's models were quite acceptable, and indeed, by now, few people seemed sure what was the current fashion.

With the return of peace came a revived interest in fashion, with gamps having a chubby look reminiscent of the 1880s and parasols being similar to the flat Japanese sunshade. In those first few post-war years it seems that more men then ever, in proportion to women, were carrying the brolly; one estimate put the ratio at four to one. Unfortunately for the trade, however, this nascent boom did not last for long and soon the umbrella was experiencing another lean period, attributed by some to the increasing number of automobiles, which, it was feared, would continue to lessen demand for the gamp. In France, umbrella manufacturers, desperately in need of publicity, appealed in a Parisian newspaper for the Prince of Wales to use a brolly: 'Carry it with ostentation, with pleasure, with affectation and with chic. The act will be copied, and soon umbrellas will again be seen in

Paris if you raise the standard in London.' In fact, the prince was already carrying an umbrella, if not with 'affectation', at least for its practical utility, for he thought it 'a characteristic convenience for a Briton'.

Women, meanwhile, were making amends for the temporary eclipse of the umbrella with a fantastic and ever-changing conglomeration of parasols, in what was to prove a magnificent swan-song of the sunshade. Every newspaper with a fashion page devoted generous space to the strange concoctions that were being evolved by the leading fashion houses and private individuals, and one can only regret that most of the contemporary illustrations, being in black and white, did scant justice to these exotic creations. Indeed, the parasol of the 'twenties was in much the same category as the Ascot hat, deliberately intended to be outrageous, even ridiculous enough to catch the camera's eye. Even so, a tradition firmly adhered to decreed that, when attending a polo match, such fripperies should be hidden away as soon as the ponies came on to the ground lest they should be frightened by the conglomerations of feathers, silk and ribbons.

In 1922 came the vogue for the canine parasol. At first it was harmless enough, the parasols merely having handles shaped like dog's heads, but when miniature models were specially made for dogs at the Pekingese and French Bulldog Clubs' exhibition at the Horticultural Hall, the 'gimmickry' had reached its zenith and the days of the parasol were numbered.

Its decline was most rapid in those countries where the sun was not excessively strong and where the shade had been carried mainly for fashion's sake. For many years the sunshade had been the more luxurious and expensive counterpart of the utility umbrella, but now a new age of sun worship was beginning, and just as the sun cult may have been responsible for the original use of parasols centuries ago, so was it now responsible for their eclipse in Europe. A sun tan was now a becoming attribute of beauty and sun lotions, not sunshades, were the means of acquiring it. Several fashion houses did, nevertheless, try to reintroduce the parasol, but though it made a small comeback in Germany in 1928, its popularity was short-lived.

Just as Britain had lagged in adopting the parasol, so was she slow to discard it. Some older women still continued to carry it on formal occasions, but a *Punch* cartoon of 1929 aptly sums up the attitudes of the two generations, with the mature woman retaining her Japanese-style shade and the girl seeking only a deep tan. *Punch* made a further comment in its summer supplement of 1934, when it showed a crowd of bronzed beach-lovers glaring at an 'anti-sunbather' muffled up and shaded by a beach-umbrella. Even as late as 1936, parasols in ivory and black georgette, and navy blue and white, were still being designed for Ascot, and when George VI and his queen visited New York in 1939, Americans regarded her then-outmoded sunshade with some astonishment.

Today, more than thirty years later, the parasol has still not quite disappeared from the English scene; the author lives in a small seaside town well-known for its many retired residents, not a few of whom may be seen holding sunshades aloft on sunny days. Ascot race meetings, too, still see the occasional parasol as a costume accessory, and sentimentalists of an older generation may display them at Buckingham Palace garden parties where, the English summer being what it is, they more often than not serve as umbrellas.

The long-neglected umbrella, taken too much for granted even by its manufacturers, could do little to fill the void left by the parasol; how could umbrellas for women remain fashionable when the first law of fashion is that nothing shall be the same for very long? Even as a utility article for men it was still not wholly acceptable socially. When Edward VIII had to go from Buckingham Palace to a meeting concerning the Duchy of Cornwall, he decided not to order his Daimler for the two-minute journey and instead walked to the Duchy offices under the protection of his umbrella, accompanied by Admiral Sir Lionel Halsey, who was similarly covered. A prowling photographer took a picture which, when published, caused a surprising amount of public disapproval, and a prominent Member of Parliament remarked to Mrs Wallis Simpson: 'That umbrella! Since you know the King, won't you ask him to be more careful in the future as to how he is photographed?'[11] Later, *The Times*, whose columns were often critical of Edward VIII, somewhat cryptically affirmed of the umbrella that 'its symbolic value [of respectability] is as high as ever; the trouble is that the thing it symbolises has declined in our estimation'.[12]

The Second World War put an almost complete stop to umbrella-manufacture and there was little that could be done to popularise them for almost a decade. The first concern of the makers in peacetime, having re-established their factories and production, was to look into the possibilities of new materials—stainless steel (which was soon judged uncommercial for ribs, but later adopted for other parts of the frame), nylon and rayon for covers. It was not until 1956 that an Umbrella Fashion Show was held, its principal theme being that no woman could really make do with less than three models—one for shopping, a long-handled type to walk with, and a third for evening use. Makers were delighted that royalty were frequently photographed using their brollies, but were still asking 'Can nothing be done to induce the Royal Family to obtain by hook or by crook a few ladies' umbrellas?' The Fashion Show proved successful and in the following year two-thirds of the models bought were carried as fashion accessories.

Umbrellas may certainly be classified as 'fashion accessories' still, but it is debatable whether they themselves have any distinct fashionable trends. The manufacturers may supply new styles, or more often re-introduce old ones, but these are soon absorbed into the miscellany of designs in use, and it is impossible to judge what is the current vogue from any cross-section of umbrella-bearers. The more colourful covers may be reckoned quite modern, and the pagoda shape is recognisable as being a fad of the mid-sixties, but that is all; no umbrella today is really out of date unless it is positively antiquated.

Certainly there is no mode in men's models, which show little individuality, and such is their durability nowadays that few men need to buy more than one or two in a lifetime. And then they are easily satisfied with any reasonably smart and efficient design. A woman may be more discriminating, but even she does not show off an umbrella as she does a new hat, nor does she buy an umbrella as often. There is, however, rather more of a fashion in umbrellas on the Continent, where parades are staged and there are even magazines devoted to the subject. Most of the modern gimmicks, such as frames incorporating cigarette-lighters or torch attachments, have also originated on the other side of the Channel, but the only one to establish itself is the modern version of the telescopic umbrella, which has also become popular in Britain.

If the umbrella is ever to become a fashion in its own right, its design will first need to become far less stereotyped than at present, no easy matter since individuality in models in these days of mass production is seldom practicable. Detachable handles, publicised in 1955, but dating back over a century, are one answer, but it is the covers which attract most attention and here there is surely scope for more adventurous designs and eye-catching colours. The best thing seen in umbrellas in many years was the Union Jack cover, in support of the 'Back Britain' campaign of 1967–8. This may not have appealed to the aesthete, but 'pop-art' even in umbrellas can do much to brighten up a wet day and at present there are all too few latter-day Hanways and MacDonalds flaunting colourful umbrellas.

8 Umbrella Lore

SINCE THE UMBRELLA'S general adoption in the western world a wealth of traditions have grown up around it. Perhaps one of the best-known of these holds that the off-duty British Guards officer is never without bowler hat and immaculately-furled brolly. Though many people on the Continent and in the United States, of course, are apt to believe that every well-dressed Englishman is thus equipped.

Today's elegant umbrella is far removed from the bulky models first used by the army during the closing years of the Napoleonic wars, when British officers sometimes carried umbrellas even when fighting; after one skirmish 'the ground was covered with sabres, satchels and umbrellas'. But their use on these occasions was not blessed with official approval. There was the famous affair on 10 December 1813, when the Grenadier Guards under Colonel Tynling occupied a redoubt outside Bayonne and several of their officers chose to shelter under umbrellas. Lord Wellington sent Arthur Hill to say that his Lordship did not approve of the use of umbrellas in action, and that he would not allow sons of gentlemen to make themselves ridiculous in the eyes of the enemy. Wellington admonished the colonel for his lax discipline the next morning, saying that Guards officers might, when on duty at St James's, carry umbrellas if they pleased, but in the field it was not only ridiculous but unmilitary. Perhaps Wellington's criticism was also a belated reflection on one of his generals, Sir Thomas Picton, who, six months previously, had ridden into battle at Vittoria with top hat, frock coat and umbrella. And the Iron Duke himself was known to use an oiled cotton umbrella which concealed a slender sword-stick.

When the allies reached Paris the following year, the French caricaturists quickly got to work on the foibles of the invaders. Number 25 in a series known as *Le Supreme Bon Ton* shows an English officer in scarlet uniform and civilian chimney-pot hat, armed with a bright green parasol against the sun. (Seven years previously Spanish troops had created a similar sensation by carrying umbrellas as they entered Hamburg.)

During the Waterloo campaign, General Mercer of the 9th Brigade, Royal Artillery, was amused by the antics of a doctor witnessing an artillery duel with an umbrella over his head. When shells started to fall near to where he stood, he decided to seek cover.

> Scarcely, however, had he made two paces when a shot, as he thought, passing rather too close, down he dropped on his hands and knees—or I should say rather hand and knees, for the one was employed in hold-ing the silken cover most pertinaciously over him—and away he scrambled like a great baboon, his head turned fearfully over his shoulder, as if watching the coming shot, whilst our fellows made the field resound with their shouts of laughter.[1]

On the opposite side, General Lejeune was equally amused to see English officers riding about in uniform holding parasols above their heads. 'The fact that they use parasols and umbrellas, though it is not the fashion in the French army, does not prevent them from being very brave soldiers.' Similar praise for the resolution displayed by '*les efféminés avec leurs parapluies*' came from Marshal Soult, who reported:

> It was raining and the English officers were on horseback, each with an umbrella in hand, which seemed to me eminently ridiculous. All at once the English closed their umbrellas, hung them on their saddles, drew their sabres, and threw themselves upon our Chausseurs.[2]

Yet Englishmen in peacetime France had been no less enter-tained at seeing members of the National Guard go to exercises with a musket in one hand and an umbrella in the other! Further-more, an officer of Napoleon's 15th Hussars had offered his sword-stick umbrella to General Alten during a wet review in 1813—though the day proved too windy for it to be held aloft.

THE TROOPS AND THE WEATHER.

Though there can be no doubt of the readiness of our gallant soldiers at all times to stand fire, it is obvious that they can't stand water. If there is to be a review, and a shower of rain comes on, our cohorts are clearly afraid of it. The idea of a weather-beaten soldier is evidently taken from the fact that a soldier is easily beaten by the weather.

As the postponement of a review is a serious disappointment to the public, we should recommend umbrellas to be added to the guns, in the same way as parasols are appended to ladies' driving whips. The experiment might be tried at all events with one regiment, who should be called the "First Parapluies." The exercise need be very simple, and "Put up umbrellas" might correspond with "Fix bayonets."

We seriously throw out this hint for the consideration of the War Office. If it is thought advisable to apply the same plan to the Cavalry, there could be a corps called the "Heavy Ginghams."

If our plan of adding umbrellas to the accoutrements of the military were to be carried out, it would be necessary to make some alterations in the martial songs of our native land; but show how easily this might be done, we subjoin a spirit-stir specimen.

March to the battle-field,
 We fear not *horrida Bella*;
Dastard is the slave who'd yield,
 Wave high the stout umbrella.

What though the foes may fly,
 As they run we'll wing 'em,
Conquer we, or bravely die:
 Unfurl, unfurl the gingham.

Base is the coward slave
 Who would turn and flee;
None but the good and brave
 Shall wield the *parapluie*.

Hence, then, with knavish fears!
 The road to glory's plain,
Whene'er that *parapluie* appears,
 Which p'rhaps will brave a thousand years
 The battle and the rain,

Troops and the Weather; *Punch's* suggestion in 1845, but one that had already been taken seriously

In the decades that followed, some Army officers doubtless continued to carry umbrellas when off duty and when the occasion demanded it, though no young officer would be so discourteous as to hold a gamp aloft if a senior officer remained unprotected nearby. Later, the habit of using an umbrella when in uniform seems to have lapsed, for George Cruikshank lightheartedly put forward the idea in 1833.[3] Twelve years later *Punch* was suggesting that umbrellas should be fixed to soldier's guns and even composed an appropriate new marching tune.

A certain colonel of the 22nd Regiment would surely have disapproved of this notion for when he saw one of his men carrying an umbrella in the 1880s he is alleged to have broken the offending article over the head of the man, who only then had a chance to explain that it belonged to his general. By then it was accepted that high-ranking officers might use umbrellas; Lord Raglan had taken a large brolly with him to the Crimea, and Field-Marshal Lord Roberts found a white parasol necessary during his Kandahar campaign while recovering from a bout of fever. General Gordon of Khartoum was another distinguished soldier who favoured the habit, and when the commander-in-chief himself, the Duke of Cambridge, was sheltered by a staff officer's umbrella during an extremely wet review, the troops were later heard to sing:

> We don't want to fight,
> But by Jingo, if we do,
> We've got the Duke of Cambridge
> And his umbrella too!

British soldiers were not alone in their attachment to the umbrella. The Boers also used them in the field in South Africa, and United States cavalrymen carried identical large cream-coloured parasols, assumedly part of their kit, at Sault-Saint-Marie, Michigan, in 1890. The unstable Louis II of Bavaria (1864–86) was particularly proud of his large umbrella, and on one occasion visited Empress Elizabeth at Possenhofen wearing his general's uniform, holding in one hand his helmet, and in the other his precious gamp. When the empress and her attendants were unable to contain their laughter, the king petulantly asked them why he should risk spoiling his *frisure*, or curly hair style. On another continent, the Chinese are said to have lost the battle of Ping Yang in 1894 to the Japanese because they were encumbered by the umbrellas they had been given in order to keep their powder dry.

Even parasols were at one time tolerated by the British Army for use by officers on active service in Asia and Africa (and notably in Aden) for they undoubtedly helped to prevent sunstroke. Not only were these shades useful against the sun, but

also in emergencies, and a number of officers, following the Duke
of Wellington's example, carried sword-stick parasols. Even an
ordinary gamp could be used as a last resort in a tight corner, as a
newspaper correspondent discovered during the Ashanti expedition of 1895–6.

In the First World War, when officers of the 6th Indian
Division were captured in Kut, they bought the entire stock of
German-made umbrellas in Baghdad, to shelter them from the
sun during their march into Asia Minor. At the same time in
Europe, marksmen in the French army were equipped with large
parasols to shade their eyes while on the firing ranges, and some
British officers carried their umbrellas on operations, where they
were useful when map-reading or message-writing in bad
weather. A. P. Le M. Sinkins found himself in a front-line
trench in apparently unceasing rain and so bought a gamp from
Armentières for 2 fr 75. Other officers followed his example so
that 'the front-line began to look like a pallid imitation of a wet
day at Ascot'. Most of them were employed during the long
periods of waiting in the trenches, but Captain Raymond Green
of the 9th Lancers carried his into action at the first Battle of
Messines.[4]

The Second World War produced no traceable umbrella
anecdotes, but was preceded in 1938 by the world's introduction
to the most notorious umbrella of the twentieth century—that
taken by Neville Chamberlain to Germany when discussing the
Munich Agreement. Though it was unlikely that he would need
to use it on his journey, it was an essential accessory for a gentleman of his generation, and as he gripped it on boarding his aircraft, it could almost be seen to exude confidence, security and
the British way of life. Decades later, the Continental nickname
for an umbrella is still 'Chamberlain', while in Britain, for those
who remember the momentous days of 1939, the word is
synonymous with bitter disillusionment.

*   *   *   *

The nineteenth century as a whole, and the first half especially,
was the age of the romantic umbrella and parasol. Women found
the sunshade a new weapon, useful for emphasising a point or to

enhance an attitude of charming reverie. A lady might decisively snap open and shoulder her parasol to denote the dismissal of an unwelcome topic or too forward an escort; or peep coyly around it at a potential suitor, and should such interest be noticed she could immediately retire behind her protective shade. As an aid to romance it featured in many tender scenes, and about 1840 J. C. Davidson even compiled a booklet of songs called *Umbrella Courtship*. True, it had been the Greek ladies of two thousand years before who had first recognised the parasol as a useful accessory in the game of love, but it was the French, as might be expected, who re-established the idea in the early nineteenth century. As Cazal so eloquently put it:

> The sunshade, like a rosy vapour, attenuates and softens the contour of the features, revives the vanished tints, surrounds the physiognomy with its diaphanous reflections. . . . How many volumes would be required to describe in its thousand fantasies the kaleidoscope of feminine thought in the use of the sunshade?
>
> Under its rosy or azure dome, sentiment buds, passion broods or blossoms; at a distance the sunshade calls and rallies to its colours, near at hand it edifies the curious eye, and disconcerts and repels presumption. How many sweet smiles have played under its corolla! How many charming signs of the head, how many intoxicating and magic looks, as the sunshade protected from jealousy and indiscretion! How many emotions, how many dramas, has it hidden with its cloud of silk![5]

In some parts of Brittany it was once the custom for a young man to invite a girl out by offering to carry her umbrella during a fair. She was then his companion for the day, and a pleasant relationship could later be continued provided the girl's parents signified their approval by inviting him to supper when he saw their daughter home. Should he carry her umbrella as they walked along the road, this was a sure sign that they were engaged. In Germany at one time, it was common for anyone distributing invitations to a wedding to carry a red umbrella, and in Hungary there was the Umbrella Dance, in which the girl held the man, who had to content himself with sheltering them both with the umbrella. In Brussels, however, it was the lady who was provided with the umbrella—and a choice of two men—in a form of cotillon dance known as *la parapluiterie*. She presented the umbrella to the one she did not wish to have as a partner, who then had to shelter his rival and the girl as they danced.

The umbrella, of course, has for long provided a convenient excuse to speak to a girl and offer its protection during a shower, and, as early as 1825, *Altberliner Redensarten* published a drawing of a lecherous-looking individual with an umbrella accosting a timorous girl in the rain. Again, in the 1880s, the French author, Uzanne, was implying that certain French 'gentlemen' armed with *parapluies* were in the habit of preying on girls (unprotected in more ways than one) on rainy evenings, and mentioned that 'many tales and novels begin with one of these Parisian meetings at a street corner on a wet evening'.[6] It was probably much the same in every city in the world.

*   *   *   *

Umbrellas are notoriously subject to being forgotten, lost, stolen, or borrowed, and once one has strayed it is seldom recovered, even though the owner may spend enough money on advertising his loss to have been able to buy a new one.

As early as 1734 a lady was announcing in the *Frankfurter Intelligenzblatt* that she had lost her green taffeta parasol trimmed with gold lace, and in 1774 an American was appealing in the *New York Journal* for the return of 'a scarlet coloured umbrella, considerably faded, but not half worn, left by a lady about four weeks ago, at some house not recollected'. There have since been innumerable such appeals in most newspapers in the world, but it was a reader of *The Times*, writing to the editor in 1868, who first appears to have discovered that umbrella-stealing had become an underworld profession:

> It has been a common practice for umbrella-stealers in the guise of female servants to answer in person advertisements for cooks, house-maids, or general servants, and to depart after having secreted an umbrella under the shawl or dress. The umbrella may be stolen either before or after the interview, according to the opportunity. I had two taken this week by two different women, who appeared about forty-five years of age; one umbrella was taken before the interview with my wife. About two years ago, precisely the same thing happened to me in another house.[7]

About the same time a gentleman reported having apprehended a thief who turned out to have eight or nine stolen umbrellas stored away, while a chaplain caught a youth who had nine pawn-tickets for stolen umbrellas. Why he should have kept the tickets for items he could surely have had no intention of redeeming is unrecorded, but he was sentenced to two months in prison.

Of the lost umbrellas, Douglas Jerrold, the well-known *Punch* humorist, is reported to have said: 'there are three things that no man but a fool lends, or having lent, is not in the most helpless state of mental crassitude if he ever hopes to get back again. These three things, my son, are books, umbrellas and money.' Ralph Waldo Emerson once remarked, when his memory for words was beginning to fail, 'I can't tell its name, but I can tell its history—strangers take it away'. And *The Times* in 1872 was sadly surmising that:

> . . . it is owing perhaps to its late introduction in Europe that men have as yet hardly recognised any distinct or separate property in umbrellas. . . . Nobody feels very guilty at taking a 'stray' umbrella if it happens to be raining as he leaves his club, or at finding himself walking home with a new umbrella, when he was conscious of having left it with an old one. . . . There are, we believe, persons eccentric enough to return umbrellas, but the instances are rare.[8]

Samuel Butler, Sir George Ferguson Bowen and an unspecified Bishop of London have each, in turn, been credited with authorship of this delightful little verse:

> The rain it raineth every day
> Upon the just and unjust fella,
> But chiefly on the just, because
> The unjust have the just's umbrella!

Running it close, is another by Dr Herbert Kynaston, canon of Durham, whose umbrella Dr Lake, the dean, had mistakenly taken from the Athenaeum:

> In Athenaeum's Hall, a sleek divine
> Left his umbrella, walking off with mine;
> So some QC takes silk and casts away
> The frayed alpaca that has seen its day.
> 'Excuse me, friend,' said he, 'a mere mistake.'
> 'A mere, indeed! You surely mean a Lake!'

History records, however, at least one person who found an umbrella no easy object to lose. This was Samuel Butler's friend, Miss Savage, who complained:

> My umbrella always comes back persistently. I have never been able to lose one; and when one, by reason of its infirmities, has become unbearable, I have to cast it loose upon Society at dead of night, or pitch it into the river. There is one of my umbrellas floating to this day in the Bay of Biscay. I set it floating down the Vilaine in the year 1867. It was seen only the year before last.[9]

Inevitably, superstitions have gathered about the umbrella and round about 1880, in Surrey and Hampshire, it was thought bad luck to open an umbrella in the house before leaving, a belief that has since spread all over Britain. More sinister is the tradition, once noted in many parts of Nebraska, that an open umbrella indoors is a certain omen of death. It is also widely believed that to place a new model over one's head, having opened it for the first time, is to invite misfortune. Another superstition, once common in the North Riding of Yorkshire, was that bad luck would come to anyone who placed an umbrella on a bed, whereas people in both Suffolk and Yorkshire thought it was tempting providence just as much to lay it on a table.

Far more pleasant is the occasional custom of toasting a person with 'Umbrellas to so-and-so', drinking their health and then inverting the emptied glasses (whose vague resemblance to umbrellas is assumed to have started the habit). But perhaps the most general superstition of all is the often-heard remark, 'If I don't take my brolly, it's bound to rain'. Robert Louis Stevenson explained it thus:

> By far the most cunning property of the umbrella is the energy which it displays in affecting the atmospheric strata. There is no act in meteorology better established—indeed, it is almost the only one on which meteorologists are agreed—than that the carriage of the umbrella produces dessication of the air; while if it be left at home, aqueous vapour is largely produced, and is soon deposited in the form of rain.[10]

Curiously enough, the umbrella has never been closely identified with St Swithin's Day, and illustrator, George Cruikshank, was one of the few to have seized on the obvious link in cartoons

George Cruikshank's comment on St Swithin's Day

he drew to commemorate the saint's day. (See illustration, page 161.) However, it may not yet be too late to establish such a tradition, as the French have shown in recently claiming St Médard's Day as the national festival of the umbrella industries. St Médard is the French equivalent of our St Swithin, and is said to have been sheltered by an eagle during a very wet day in the fifth century. Now French manufacturers use his feast day to express the unity and prosperity of their trade, the day's proceedings including a church service, a mannequin parade, and a dinner.

A less worthy tradition, and one which has happily now disappeared, was that the umbrella was an emblem of snobbery, and that to carry a gamp was to proclaim oneself a cut above the rest. Certainly this was true enough of the 1870s, when the umbrella had become an index of social position, a man being judged by the type he carried. Delicate frame, choice silk, polished Malacca cane with silver mounting inscribed with name and address, 'tell me if *that* could be carried by anyone but a gentleman!'

Gradations of class were infinite, ranging from the above splendid example to 'the tattered and dingy rags which, hanging from a few bent wires, make a poor attempt to shelter the ill-clad form of shivering humanity'. Thus the Victorians paid great heed to their umbrellas, so that when thin, furled silk umbrellas were *à la mode* 'a person carrying a cotton umbrella curiously enough has just borrowed it from a friend'. When Sabine Baring-Gould visited Innsbruck in the 1870s he bought an umbrella

> ... of a brilliant red, and imprinted round it was a wreath of flowers and foliage, white, yellow, blue and green; around the ferrule also was a smaller wreath similar in colour and character. This cover was stretched on canes, such canes as are well-known in schools; and the canes were distended by twisted brass strainers, rising out of a solid tube of elaborately hammered brass, through which passed the stick of the umbrella. The whole, when expanded, measured nearly five feet, and was not extraordinarily heavy, nothing like the weight of a gig-umbrella. ...
>
> I reached Heidelberg, on my way home, and innocently walked with it under my arm in the Castle Gardens on Sunday afternoon. Then I found that it provoked attention and excited astonishment. Such an umbrella had its social level, and that level was the market-place, not the Castle Gardens; it was sufferable as spread over an old woman

vending *sauerkraut*, but not as carried furled in the hand of a re-
spectably-dressed gentleman. So much comment did my umbrella
occasion that it annoyed me, spoiled the pleasure of my walk.[11]

The only umbrellas exempt from the rules of social distinction
were those borne by doctor or parson, whose gamps were conceded to be necessary to their calling. Their utilitarian brollies
commanded respect if not admiration, and one tradesman in
1872 introduced the Clerical Umbrella, whose 'stout, ebony
handle and serviceable alpaca marks at a glance the decorous
hard-working parson'. The idea was apparently inspired by an
Archbishop of Canterbury, John Sumner, 'famous for walking
across Westminster Bridge to the opening of Parliament with a
cotton umbrella, and we at once recognise the temper and
theology of the man'.

Towards the end of the century, the number of different
umbrellas indicative of social levels began to decrease, and today
there remains only the more or less standard umbrella, with,
exceptionally, a few splendid models to indicate the opulence of
their privileged owners. Nevertheless the carrying of a umbrella
still seems to irk some members of the community who appear
to think it is being carried only out of pretentiousness. Perhaps
this was the reason behind the phenomenon that was puzzling
readers of *The Times* in 1957—why did bus drivers persistently
ignore the waving of a raised umbrella as a request to halt their
bus? Was it, they speculated, due to some social susceptibility
over the humility of one man serving another, and the raised
umbrella being 'a mark of undemocratic class imperiousness'?[12]

Perhaps the simple answer was just that bus conductors had
become thoroughly tired of collecting all the gamps which were
left on their vehicles; more than 70,000 of which were found on
buses and trains in London alone that year. And, of course, the
drivers themselves had no doubt long forgotten, if they ever
knew, that their predecessors on the open Metropolitan buses in
the 1880s were provided with large red umbrellas.

9 *The Umbrella in Literature and the Arts*

O VER THE CENTURIES the umbrella has intrigued numerous writers, both of fact and fiction, and a number of these have already been cited in this history. A few only have written complete works on the subject, but many others have contributed relevant information in articles or sections of books. Both passing references and lengthy passages are plentiful in foreign literature, and many date back well beyond the advent of printing. British references, however, start in the sixteenth century, and since then have appeared in moderation, if not abundance. It is in English literature, too, that there is described the most famous fictional umbrella of all, the one which Daniel Defoe's hero, Robinson Crusoe, constructed, notwithstanding that he had just completed 'a great cap for my head, with the hair on the outside to shoot off the rain':

> After this, I spent a great deal of time and pains to make me an umbrella; I was indeed in great want of one, and had a great mind to make one; I had seen them made in the Brazils, where they were very useful in the great heats which are there; and I felt the heats every jot as great here . . . it was a most useful thing to me, as well for the rains as the heats. I took a world of pains at it, and was a great while before I could make anything likely to hold; nay, after I thought I had hit the way, I spoiled two or three before I made one to my mind; but at last I made one that answered indifferently well; the main difficulty I found was to make it let down. I could make it spread, but if it did not let down too, and draw in, it was not portable for me any way but just over my head, which would not do. However, at last, as I said, I made one to answer, and covered it with skins, the hair upwards, so that it cast off the rain like a pent-house, and kept off the sun so

effectually that I could walk out in the hottest of the weather with greater advantage than I could before in the coolest; and when I had no need for it, could close it and carry it under my arm.[1]

For almost 200 years after the publication of Defoe's book in 1719, 'Robinson' was a popular name for any umbrella in France, and few illustrators dared to omit it from their representations of Crusoe; nor could anyone appear as the castaway at a fancy dress ball without a shade of skins. Robert Louis Stevenson summed up its fascination when he commented that Crusoe's 'leaf-umbrella is as fine an example of the civilised mind striving to express itself under adverse circumstances as we have ever met with'.[2]

Prior to 1800, the only work entirely devoted to umbrellas was Paulus Paciaudus's *De Umbellae Gestatione*, a learned and well-researched tract in Latin. The first British book on the subject was an anonymous dissertation on the umbrella's significance in the Athenian Skiraphoria, which proved to be a rambling and unenlightening account.[3] In the same year that this was published—1801—J. S. Duncan issued his *Hints to the Bearers of Walking Sticks and Umbrellas*, which, as its title implies, was a form of instruction manual. It confirms the impression given in contemporary satirical engravings that many people had little idea how to handle their umbrellas. There was such a demand for Duncan's book that it ran into a third edition, but it is now so scarce and exceedingly difficult to obtain that it is, perhaps, worth quoting some of the quainter passages at length:

Every one who has ever walked through the crowded streets of any town must have met with considerable obstruction and annoyance from the awkward manner in which the greater part of mankind carry both Walking Sticks and Umbrellas. . . . One man, a gentleman, not wilfully rude, not malicious, but without reflection, dips his cane into the mud, and then wipes the dirty ferrule on the clean dress of the next woman who passes. Another twirls his stick in the air, though sure to strike someone near him, or to jerk the dirt over the backs and faces of passengers before and behind. A third flexes his cane or umbrella underneath his arm: if he move straight forward, the ferrule behind impales the eye of one who follows with a brisker step; or if it should slope downward, stabs his breast or soils his dress. If the bearer of the stick so placed turn himself sideways in the street, he becomes a sort of turnstile; his stick extends over the whole pavement, the near-sighted are struck in the neck or face, and all are obliged to move around it or remonstrate.[4]

Duncan categorises umbrella-bearers into 'Shield-Bearers, Sky-Strikers, Mud-Scoopers, Inverters or Self-Tormentors' and details, with the aid of diagrams, how they might handle 'Umbrellas as seem most convenient to the ease of the walker, and least likely to incommode the public':

A word or two on expanded Umbrellas. The Shield-Bearer drives his Umbrella before him, covering completely his head and body. He can see no-one in front and he occupies the whole pavement: he either runs against every one before him, or compels them to step into the gutter. If, however, he should meet with an Unicorn [He who carries his walking-stick so that 'his formidable horn projects and forces a passage through the crowd for the resolute charge.'] the Cane of the latter pierces and rends the silk or varnished cover of the Umbrella. Thus rival follies and contending vices mutually annoy each other to the furtherance of justice, and to the advantage of the community. Every reader of the *Morning Post* and *Morning Chronicle* is of course acquainted with the dislocation of Lady Jasey's tete by Dr Sheldrake's Umbrella. Her Ladyship's connections with the ministry, and the Doctor's with some leading men of the opposition, having involved the affair in all the fury of political party, I shall abstain from offering an opinion on so delicate a subject, especially as it is likely to be farther agitated in Westminster Hall. When two passengers meet and wish to pass with spread Umbrellas, each should incline his pole in the angle 45 to his proper side; thus neither will be incommoded. . . . When two meet a third, the centre should elevate, and the outside slope, umbrellas. The generality are Sky-Strikers or Mud-Scoopers. Every passer either jerks up his Umbrella to the sky, wherby the shorter endangers with the points of his whalebone the eyes of the taller, or dashes it to the ground so as to impede all passage: the latter case is the last degree of awkwardness, and chiefly occurs amongst the most vulgar servant-maids and young children. These are called Mud-Scoopers, from plunging the edge of their instrument by such means into the dirt.

Inverters are those careless beings who present the inside of the Umbrella to the wind, whereby the cover is turned inside out, and commonly much lacerated, while they impede the progress of many a time-pressed citizen, during the awkward attempts to re-arrange it.[5]

Duncan was in no doubt as to how the problem should be solved:

Carrying umbrellas, 1801; An Inverter, Sky-Striker and Mud-Scooper

. . . common sense, and a small degree of sympathy with general distress, points out an easy method of avoiding all the above disorders, viz, that the cane or closed umbrella should be borne as close to the body, as near to the front, as possible, and constantly in a perpendicular position.[6]

The first of what was to become a long string of informative articles on the umbrella was anonymously contributed to *The Penny Magazine* in 1835. It was apparently inspired by the author having been threatened by a sentry for not dipping his umbrella in respect as he passed the palace of the Sultan of Turkey. Some of the information given in earlier articles reappears in subsequent contributions, garnished with new facts which the authors have gleaned for themselves.[7]

One of the most impressive of the early works was a laudatory opus by René-Marie Cazal (but probably 'ghosted' by Charles Marchal). Cazal was a well-known French manufacturer and umbrella-maker to Louis Philippe's queen and then to Empress Eugenie, wife of Napoleon III—political dexterity indeed. The book set the style for successive publications, its rhetoric contrasting oddly with so prosaic a subject; there was for instance an eulogistic tribute to 'the dauntless mariners' who procured the whalebone needed for umbrella ribs.[8]

In 1845, G. H. Rodwell's illustrated novel *Memoirs of an Umbrella* was published, and very soon forgotten. It tells of the experiences of an umbrella from the time it is sold in a shop at St Martin's Court, London, to the day it is closed for the last time. The story, though tolerably interesting, contributes little to this study, apart from an interesting title-page.

Charles Dickens played a special part in fostering the Victorians' interest in 'brolliology', and introduced into his novels the concept of treasured models. He also contributed a new word to the language when he created Mrs Gamp in *Martin Chuzzlewit*; the disreputable nurse soon gave her name to any untidy loose umbrella, for she was never without 'a species of gig-umbrella; the latter article in colour like a faded leaf except where a circular patch of a lively blue had been dexterously let in at the top'. At home, the battered object 'as something of great price and rarity was displayed with particular ostentation'. When

Title-page from *Memoirs of an Umbrella*, which confirms
the Victorians' interest in the umbrella

she travelled to Hertfordshire in a coach, her umbrella was 'particularly hard to be got rid of, and several times thrust out its battered brass nozzle from improper crevices and chinks, to the great terror of other passengers'.

Dickens also made several allusions to other models, the one for instance with which Squeers so unkindly belaboured Smike, and Mrs Mowcher's great umbrella in *David Copperfield*.[9] Furthermore, he printed an informative article in his magazine *Household Words* giving details of the manufacturing practice of the period.[10] This was based to some extent on *The Report of the Juries*, published the year after the Great Exhibition, and which, besides describing and commenting on the umbrellas on display, gave an excellent history with useful references to other sources.

Two of Dickens' illustrators, William Thackeray and George Cruikshank, also paid some attention to the umbrella and featured it humorously in their engravings. *Punch*, too, has always been very fond of the umbrella, which has appeared in many of its cartoons, sometimes as the principal subject. Other Victorian periodicals, notably the *Illustrated London News* and *Graphic*, feature honorific parasols in scenes of foreign lands, though the drawings require some finding in the now mouldy and heavily-bound volumes.

In 1855, manufacturer William Sangster wrote his *Umbrellas and their History*, giving his own version of well-known anecdotes. Some of these had originally appeared in the recently established *Notes & Queries*, whose readers eagerly wrote in to give literary references to the umbrella dating back many years. The quotations most frequently cited as the earliest were those from Swift and Gay and, unfortunately, as a new generation of readers appeared, they mostly reiterated the discoveries of the original correspondents.

Other well-known authors who have expressed affection for the gamp include Samuel Butler, the poet Fitz Greene Halleck, and Isaac D'Israeli.[11] One popular writer was himself a manufacturer; this was Joseph Wright who made the famous 'Drooko' umbrellas at Glasgow between 1885 and 1912. A noted lay preacher and philanthropist, he also wrote Scots prose and poetry, his *Scenes of Scottish Country Life* achieving a circulation of 30,000 copies. So renowned were his umbrellas that Professor Stuart Blackie wrote of them:

> I walk the world a raintight fellow
> Beneath the Joseph Wright umbrella.

Wright published many of his own works and so was able to include advertisements for his products, one of his books devoting no less than twelve pages to them.[12]

From manufacturer to user, and what more eulogistic tribute could be paid by an umbrella-owner than this from George Borrow?

Rain came on, but it was at my back, so I expanded my umbrella, flung it over my shoulder and laughed. Oh, how a man laughs who has a good umbrella when he has the rain at his back, aye and over his head too, and at all times when it rains except when the rain is in his face, when the umbrella is not of much service. Oh, what a good friend to a man is an umbrella in rain time, and likewise at many other times. What need he fear if a wild bull or a ferocious dog attacks him, provided he has a good umbrella? He unfurls the umbrella in the face of the bull or dog, and the brute turns around quite scared, and runs away. Or if a footpad asks him for his money, what need he care provided he has an umbrella? He threatens to dodge the ferrule into the ruffian's eye, and the fellow starts back and says 'Lord, sir! I meant no harm, I never saw you before in all my life. I merely meant a little fun.' Moreover, who doubts that you are a respectable character provided you have an umbrella? You go into a public-house and call for a pot of beer, and the publican puts it down before you with one hand, without holding out the other for the money, for he sees that you have an umbrella and consequently property. And what respectable man, when you overtake him on the way and speak to him, will refuse to hold conversation with you, provided you have an umbrella? No one. The respectable man sees that you have an umbrella and concludes that you do not intend to rob him, and with justice, for robbers never carry umbrellas. Oh, a tent, a shield, a lance and a voucher for character is an umbrella. Amongst the very best of friends of man must be reckoned an umbrella.

(As the umbrella is rather a hackneyed subject, two or three things will, of course, be found in the above eulogium on an umbrella which have been said by other folks on that subject; the writer, however, flatters himself that in his eulogium on an umbrella, two or three things will also be found which have never been said by anyone else about an umbrella.)[13]

From its earliest adoption into the English language, the

word 'umbrella' was a commonly used metaphor for any form of shelter or protection, and there are numerous Victorian examples of this usage. In 1840, Bishop Edward Stanley visited Oxford University, where his son was enjoying great academic success. Because of his politics, evident from his speeches in the House of Lords, the bishop had been somewhat apprehensive as to his reception. 'I expected' he said, 'to receive a pitiless storm, but under my son's umbrella, I got well through'.[14] Again, when Rowland Hill was preaching in chapel, many people came in to shelter from the rain. Hill observed: 'My brethren, I have often heard that religion can be made a cloak, but this is the first occasion on which I ever knew it could be converted into an umbrella.'[15] (In fact, Francis Osborne had used the word in a similar context some two hundred years earlier when he referred to 'Those brain-sick fools, as did oppose the discipline and ceremonies of the church and made religion an umbrella to impiety'.[16])

On 6 July 1885, Lord Salisbury announced at the annual meeting of the Liberal party that 'we are all content to stand under Mr Gladstone's umbrella', and for a while the gamp was the accepted symbol of party union. Somebody even published a book of election lyrics called *Under the Umbrella, or, The Grand Old Man's Garland of Election Lyrics*—to which *Punch's* somewhat acid comment was a cartoon depicting a distinctly battered umbrella. (See opposite.)

Modern writers, understandably enough, have contributed little to the literature of the umbrella, an honourable exception being A. G. Gardiner who wrote a delightful essay 'On Umbrella Morals'. In it he comments on straying gamps (comparing them to books and hats in this respect) and describes with awe 'a super-umbrella' that had found its way into his house, and which belonged to 'a certain statesman'.[17]

In much the same sort of vein, *The Times* has printed several light leaders on umbrellas, as well as various letters on mishandling and losing them. In December 1930, the same newspaper published a series of letters on the subject of lost umbrellas, and followed this in October 1934 with anecdotes about the umbrella in wartime. The long-defunct *Daily News* also

THE OLD UMBRELLA.

Gladstone. " My Umbrella wants re-covering."   *Chamberlain.* " Step inside, Sir. Re-cover it while you wait."

The Old Umbrella; a *Punch* cartoon of 1885 satirising the
metaphorical umbrella of Mr Gladstone

showed considerable interest in the gamp and published many
letters in the later months of 1929 following the theme 'Dear Sir,
I have had my umbrella for forty years, is this a record?'

More recently *The Observer* carried an article, 'Put Up More
Gamps', in which Ivor Brown made this original plea on behalf
of mountaineers:

Especially would I plead for really powerful umbrellas to be used
in the climbing of mountains, where rain is not unknown. Rolled, it
would be a good staff, unfolded a genuine shelter, except in cases of high

LONDON LAUGHS   (No. 6,336)   *By LEE*

"Our Borough Sanitary Officer has been greatly impressed by the colourful pageantry of local functionaries in Nigeria."

London Laughs: one unusual example of the Britisher's occasional awareness of the foreign state umbrella

wind, when it too easily becomes a parachute in reverse—I have
myself stormed Snowdonia's Siabod, umbrella in hand, but my prop,
being a weakling, snapped. Hence my demand for a climber's umbrella
as strictly durable as the club of Hercules.[18]

Of more permanent value are several lengthy accounts, some
of them scholarly in their approach, which have been published
in the present century—at the rate of one a decade! These have
originated overseas and are not conveniently obtainable by the
British reader, but two, by Max von Boehn and A. Varron, have
been translated into English.

*   *   *   *

Even in architecture the umbrella has found a place, thanks
to an early nineteenth-century enthusiast who built himself an
Umbrella Cottage at Lyme Regis, in Dorset. It still stands, a
most desirable residence high above the town, of polygonal
design, with a central chimney and the thatch trimmed in the
shape of an umbrella cover. (See illustration, page 125.) Earlier
still, in the eighteenth century, the umbrella had given its name
to the roofed structures with open sides that were sometimes
placed at the ends of walks in gardens.

Statues which incorporate an umbrella include those of Sir
William Waterlow in Waterlow Park, Highgate, and George
William Palmer, of Huntley & Palmer fame, in Palmer Park,
Reading. It has been stated that Richard Cobden's statue in
Manchester includes an umbrella, but this is not the case. In
1852, C. A. Davis wrote to the New York poet, Fitz Greene
Halleck, expressing a wish to commemorate him with a monument in his lifetime, and asking 'Have you any special objection
to an umbrella under your arm? . . . If it is not there, the likeness
will not strike'. The poet, whose affection for his umbrella was
well-known, was amused by the suggestion, but when a statue
was erected—posthumously—the umbrella was omitted.[19]

A form of umbrella monument was planned at Omaha,
Nebraska, when that town was preparing for its Trans-Mississippi
Exposition of 1898; it was designed to stand 350 ft high, and
had a car attached to each 'rib' so that the whole affair would
hold 350 people.

By a mechanical arrangement worked by electric power, visitors who enter the cars will find themselves gradually ascending, for the gigantic umbrella will open in the same way as the ordinary portable article, and when the cars are at their greatest height, the whole super-structure of ribs will revolve around the central shaft. This extra-ordinary attraction is now being constructed, and it will certainly form one of the greatest engineering feats of the century. Further, it will form a fitting monument of that great, though inanimate, friend of mankind, the umbrella.[20]

At one time the umbrella trade were considering the erection of a monument to Jonas Hanway, as the British pioneer of the umbrella, but though nothing came of this idea Hanway is com-memorated by having a street named after him in London and by a memorial in the west aisle of the north transept of West-minster Abbey.

*   *   *   *

A matter of some regret to its connoisseurs is that the um-brella has not yet been generally accorded the status of antique. True that the parasol has been classed as 'a small antique' in one modern work, written by Therle Hughes,[21] but one comprehen-sive encyclopaedia on antiques, which even includes sections on buttons, pipes, walking-sticks, shawls and fans, makes no reference to umbrellas or parasols!

Occasionally, early models or ones of special interest are sold at auction, mainly to individual collectors, but Christie's, for instance, find that they bring very little unless fitted with ex-tremely fine handles. In 1967, four ordinary Victorian parasols made but six guineas; next year four handles alone, decorated with gold and pearl, sold for fifty-eight guineas.

Fortunately, there are several private collections of parasols—that belonging to Mrs Mary Ireland being exceptional—and most large museums have a selection of both sunshades and umbrellas, usually as part of the fashion collection. The London Museum, in particular, is well worth a visit, as there one may see the umbrellas of George IV, the chain-mail parasol of Queen Vic-toria, and another royal gamp, believed to be that of Edward VII when Prince of Wales. There are also various less distinguished umbrellas dating back from the nineteenth century, including quite an early model bearing the initials of one, Thomas Pease. It is solid and square in section, with dark brown twilled silk with satin border fitted to whalebone ribs.

The Victoria and Albert Museum has a few examples of large silk umbrellas and a representative selection of other models, including Lady Elizabeth Waldgrave's parasol dated *circa* 1865, with a silk insertion representing brightly coloured butterflies. The Gallery of English Costume at Platt Hall, Manchester, has over 200 models, most of which are parasols, and Birmingham's Museum about fifty. Few examples preserved today date before 1840, though Snowshill Manor in Worcestershire has some early designs amongst its fifty models, as well as a dozen huge Victorian carriage-umbrellas.

A number of European museums also have comprehensive ranges on the same lines as British collections, usually including many parasols and a smaller number of umbrellas, but few have any noteworthy associations. There is a specialist collection at the Museo dell' Ombrello e del Parasole, rather remotely situated at Gignese, near Stresa. Every family in this village was once engaged in the umbrella trade, and a fine collection of umbrellas has been accumulated. Of special interest to English visitors is a letter concerning Neville Chamberlain's umbrella; in 1938 the museum asked if they might have the model the Prime Minister had taken to Munich. The reply was terse:

Dear Sir,   8 November 1938
    I am writing on behalf of the Prime Minister to express regret that because of very many similar requests he is unable to do what you ask.
                                        Yours Truly,
                                            E. M. WATSON.

Now framed and prominently displayed, the letter is one of the museum's treasures, together with such notable exhibits as the umbrella of the Doge of Venice, and that of a chief constable of Turin, who favoured an 8-in dagger incorporated in the stick.

Most of the major American museums have extensive collections, with numerous examples of the parasol being displayed as costume accessories, rather than forming a display in their own right. The Essex Institute at Salem, Massachusetts, has over

L

200 examples, though the collection is somewhat neglected; it contains one or two umbrellas dating back over two centuries, several of the earliest English export models, *circa* 1790, and a Paris-made parasol that was paid for with $60 worth of gold in about 1862. The Museum of the City of New York has 275 models, some of which belonged to people of local repute. There seems to be more interest in the history of the umbrella in America than in Britain, though little mystique surrounds its everyday use across the Atlantic, and there is a paucity of bibliographic material.[22]

Often under the same roof as the actual models are paintings featuring the umbrella. Besides those older works of art mentioned in earlier chapters, there are various other well-known paintings dominated by the umbrella or sunshade. Works of Tiepolo, Dubuffet, Degas, Monet and Goya include one or other of the two; Renoir's *The Umbrellas* hangs in the National Portrait Gallery; Tissot's *The Sunshade*, and Ford Madox Brown's *The Last of England* (which features a very utilitarian umbrella sheltering a family leaving the country) are displayed in the Birmingham Art Gallery. Delacroix included the royal umbrella of Morocco in his portrait of Mouley Abd-er Rahman, and Canaletto featured that of the Doge of Venice. The umbrella is most frequently seen, however, in examples of Oriental art where, as has been noted, it is often an item of special significance.

10 *The Umbrella Industry*

U MBRELLA TRADERS BEGAN to flourish in Britain in the last quarter of the eighteenth century, when the demand for umbrellas for the first time warranted a home industry. Previously, marketing had been limited to a handful of firms who received much of their stock from overseas. But as the trend became popular an increasing number of merchants began to sell, and eventually to manufacture for themselves, umbrellas and parasols. In 1779, one James Watson supplied Titus Hibbert with an umbrella for £1 10s, and then made two more models for a mere £1. In the following year Mark Bull took out the first patent for umbrellas in this country, though his idea was actually for 'a machine for supporting an umbrella which may be fixed to any saddle or wheeled carriage', the purpose being to leave the driver's hands free to hold the reins of the horse. The design survived for at least twenty years, which was a great deal longer than the average period of popularity enjoyed by subsequent umbrella gimmicks conjured up by hopeful inventors.

Kent's Directory of London listed some of these early manufacturers, and in 1781 noted Saxby & Golding, who had an 'Oil'd Silk, Linen and Umbrella Warehouse' at 32 St Martin's-le-Grand. There are also early references to makers in the Birmingham directories, which in 1785 list Robert Gill, umbrella-maker, of Lady Wood Lane, and Michael Lawrence, stick umbrella and angle-rod maker, of 54 Bull Street.

Some of the work of these early traders relied rather too much on trial and error, and other people's designs. Round about 1786, John Gardner of Glasgow attempted to manufacture an umbrella

which was perhaps inspired by the one introduced into the city
by Dr Jamieson four years earlier.

> It was indeed a very clumsy article. The cloth was heavy oil or wax-
> glazed linen, and the ribs were formed of Indian cane, such as shortly
> before this time ladies were accustomed to use as hoops to extend
> their petticoats. The handle was massive and strong, and altogether
> it was a load to carry. Mr Gardner was obliged to give up his manu-
> facture as the Manchester people had been able to make a lighter
> article and at a cheaper rate.[1]

Few of the small one-man concerns grew into anything larger
(though several family businesses were very successful), for, like
John Gardner, they were faced with powerful, if irregular, competition from larger firms which included the umbrella as just
one of their many lines. A typical example was Owen Owens
& Son of Manchester. Originally hat-lining cutters and glazers,
they saw the potential of the new industry, and in 1810 began to
make their own models, buying the components from Rubery &
Barrs of Birmingham. Within three years they were steadily
selling models covered in silk and cotton gingham, the latter
being a glossy cotton fabric, like linen, named after the town of
Guingamp in Brittany. It was also a popular name for an umbrella covered with the material. Owen Owens used the popular
method of employing workers at home, which obviated the need
for extensive factory facilities, and allowed an unprofitable trade
to be abandoned without incurring heavy loss. As it happened,
the demand for whalebone (still the main commodity for ribs at
this period) caused its price to double in 1822–3, and the firm,
worried by the high cost, suspended umbrella manufacture in
December 1822.

Other firms tried to sidestep this problem by using wood,
cane, or even wire-threaded osier twigs for ribs, but none of these
substitutes was wholly satisfactory. Owen Owens themselves
later resumed production by fitting longer metal tips to the
ribs, using 26 in of whalebone for a 28-in rib. In 1825, however,
when the price of whalebone went even higher, they had first to
reduce their output, then finally to abandon the actual manufacture of umbrellas. But the firm still retained stocks of runners
and other components until 1846, and continued to export

A Great variety of Table Mats and Doyleys

T. POWER

Bathing Caps and Hat Covers

WHOLESALE · Retail For · EXPORTATION

Umbrella, Parasol &

Furniture

MANUFACTURER

N.43 Bull Street Birmingham

The Trade

Supplied

with all kinds of Materials.

Advertisement of an umbrella wholesaler, 1821; many
businesses carried other lines besides umbrellas and parasols

umbrellas to Rio de Janeiro, Pernambuco and the Cape of Good
Hope, as well as supplying them to John Robinson of Baltimore.[2]

Most of the smaller firms had no choice but to struggle on, and
eventually the majority managed to overcome their difficulties.
At the end of the Napoleonic wars there were some sixty-three
umbrella businesses in London, and eighteen in Manchester.
Wrightson's New Triennial Directory for 1818 lists only eight
names under 'Umbrella and Parasol Makers' in Birmingham, but
already several well-known trade names had established them-

selves in that city, including Joseph Rubery, Thomas Holland, and his partner-to-be, William Cox.

The large number of one-man concerns and the cursory manufacture of umbrellas gave the trade little solidarity or unity, and it was not until the 1840s that it became recognised outside its own limited circles. Prior to this date, it is conspicuous only by its absence from statistical returns and accounts of early nineteenth-century commerce. One may guess that the general hotchpotch of firms made the figures hard to gather, though other, comparable, industries are featured in such detailed works as *Tables of the Revenue, Population, Commerce &c of the United Kingdom and its Dependencies, 1820–43*, in which the umbrella-trade is completely ignored, as is the case in *The Book of Trades* of 1846, which lists almost every other calling imaginable.

The home trade finally merited recognition when, thanks to its massive production of ordinary cheap umbrellas, it established a position rivalled only by that of France. Britain had the advantage of importing free of duty the various basic materials—canes, whalebones, horn and ivory—from her colonies, and of possessing a flourishing textile industry at home, capable of providing covering material, and, incidentally, reducing the French production of gingham. By 1851, London had about 1,330 workers in the trade, a third of whom were in the Stepney area, and many of whom were women doing dull and dirty work. There were various large firms in northern towns, and countless small manufacturers all over the country; the score of umbrella-makers in Devon, for instance, were mainly one-man concerns.

By comparison, Paris in 1847 had 377 makers with 1,429 employees (with women in the majority) producing goods valued at £296,320. The output value for France as a whole was over £400,000, a fifth of which went abroad. (This is slightly less than a reasonable estimate for British exports at this time.) Furthermore, the country had ninety-six specialists making the sticks and twenty-nine workshops making the rest of the frames. Such a low average of under four workers per factory was quite common—Prussia had seventy-seven factories with a staff of 500, and in Saxony forty-five firms employed but ninety-one people.[3]

A quick analysis of the number of patents taken out in Britain during this period confirms the impression that the industry had found its feet by mid-century; twenty-six patents were filed between 1780 and 1840, seventeen in the 1840s, and a massive 123 in the 1850s. Many of these were mere gimmicks, often the brainwaves of people with no trade connections, but they did include a proportion of sound improvements in ordinary design, the result of work by such men as Samuel Fox, the most outstanding of all home manufacturers, who is said to have made £300,000 out of his enterprises in steel. Fox was originally a Derbyshire wire-drawer who took over a disused cotton-mill in the South Yorkshire village of Stocksbridge in 1842. At first, he limited his production to making wire for crinolines, and pins for wool combing, but then began to venture into the production of umbrella frames, hitherto almost monopolised by Birmingham men.

Very soon, Fox had registered a design at the Patent Office for an improved steel rib, with the claim that 'Nothing equal to it has ever yet been brought out'. Certainly it seemed neater and stronger than previous designs, though Henry Holland had taken out an earlier patent for a tubular type rib in 1840, and Pierre Duchamp of Lyons had a similar idea six years later. But Fox was the first successfully to exploit the steel rib, and in 1849 was buying 'No 1 tubes, iron runners and iron notches' from Thomas Cox of Birmingham, and producing his own frames at Stocksbridge, where he started production of his own U-section steel ribs in 1852. Holland and Duchamp opposed his request for a patent, for the ideas of all three were very similar, but Fox finally secured one as from 6 April 1852.[4]

Duchamp patented his own flute ribs in France, while Holland doubtless took consolation from the award of a prize medal for his frames at the Great Exhibition; his own rectangular steel tubing reduced the weight of a silk-covered umbrella to 9 oz, but put the cost up by 2s. At first, none of the ribs produced by the three rivals attracted much enthusiasm commercially, for they had many imitators (notwithstanding the patents) producing inferior work, and it took several years for it to be generally agreed that the new design was preferable to the old whalebones.

The industrial event of the era was the Great Exhibition of 1851, which not only included a display of many types of umbrella, but also resulted in the publication, in *The Report of the Juries*, of a useful international survey that compared the products of different countries, often unfavourably, with those of Britain. But full justice was done to the work of the French manufacturers.

> In the higher class of umbrellas and parasols, France undoubtedly stands pre-eminent. The tasteful designs and sharp and excellent carving of the ivory handles, and the artistic grouping of the colours of the various silks used in the manufacture of parasols, and the supple dressing of the silks for umbrellas, give to the French manufactures a decided superiority; added to which, the frames were much lighter and neater than those made in England until a very recent period. The French parasols and umbrellas have, in consequence of their lightness and elegance, acquired a high reputation in America and Italy. . . . [But] the productions of France must be characterised as high in price; the ordinary wholesale price of a good silk umbrella of the self-opening construction ranges from 20s to 40s, and that of parasols from 13s to 80s; but then they are in every respect exquisitely finished.[5]

When the Juries came to judge the exhibits of the United Kingdom, they reckoned 'England is without a rival in the production of parsols and umbrellas of the plainer descriptions'. But the most expensive lace and silk parasol on view, at five guineas,

> . . . was far less elegant than most of the specimens in the French Department, and much higher in price. Our umbrella manufacturers would, indeed, do well to profit by the example of their French brethren, by calling artistic talent to their aid in devising new models. For there are many English artists who are capable of furnishing excellent designs for the ivory carver, and of superintending the carving of the first model; with whose aid we should gradually find good engraving taking the place of its present substitute, high polish, whilst the cost on each individual article would be very slightly increased. A little artistic help is likewise desirable in the assortment of harmonious tints; and at the next Exhibition, there will be no examples of crimson parasols with yellow fringes.[6]

Of the thirty-three exhibitors, five were awarded prize medals, and two obtained honourable mentions. Among the medallists was the Parisian manufacturer, E. Charageat, who was commended for his first-rate workmanship; the jury found his design and sculpturing of handles of the highest class and also noted his 'numerous examples of ingenious mechanical contrivances'. René-Marie Cazal won his medal for similar reasons, though his prices were very high, between 32s and 100s. English successes in prize medals were gained by Holland, the Sangster brothers, and J. Morland & Son of Eastcheap, whose parasols and umbrellas were 'of very excellent workmanship and at moderate prices'; his umbrellas cost from 3s 6d to 22s, and silk parasols from 1s 7d up to 16s.

The Report of the Juries also drew attention to the prosperous condition of the British industry, and although confessing its inability to determine any figures for yearly production, gave an interesting account of constructional methods and prices. The mid-century frame-maker required a couple of simple lathes, one of which would be fitted with a circular saw; a rose-cutter for forming the tips of the ribs; several drills, which screwed into the mandrils of the lathes; also a paring knife, a small vice, and various other commonplace tools such as pliers. All these would cost between £3 and £6.

To assemble an eight-ribbed frame took what was variously estimated at 135 or 163 successive operations, yet the piece-work pay was pitifully small, being ½d to ¾d for a parasol frame, ¾d to 1d for a cane-ribbed umbrella, and 2½d for one with whalebone ribs. The industry was then using 400 tons of whalebone fins each year, as well as a growing amount of steel for the new-type ribs. A workman with four boy assistants could make 600 cheap frames a week to earn, perhaps, 50s. But sheet brass and iron wire cost 8s, and each boy was paid 4s in wages. So a workman might make 24s or 26s a week, 'but he is frequently subjected to much loss by being kept about in the wholesale warehouses, which sometimes occasions the loss of at least half a day to him'.

Once a frame had been manufactured in the workshop, it was 'put out' to a needlewoman, either working regularly at the warehouse, or more spasmodically in her own home. She would stitch the gores (the sections of covers) together at the rate of 1s a dozen for the cheapest types, or 4s for the best. The art of sewing without ever taking the little steel needle out of the seam, drawing the thread the whole way through and finally scraping the seam down with the thumbnail was termed 'tweedling'. The edges were then hemmed (one firm, Lewis & Allenby of Regent Street began to pink the edges in 1851, rather than hem them, to prevent fraying) and the whole cover was tacked to the frame. The ferrule and handle were then fitted, usually back at the warehouse, and the umbrella was ready for sale. Since the piece-work rate paid for these jobs was so low, and regular workers suffered from business falling off after November, the work was aptly described as 'slavery for one half of the year, and starvation for the other half'.

Because of the low labour costs, a child's gingham cost only 4d, a woman's gingham or small silk parasol 10½d, and a gingham umbrella, weighing perhaps 8 oz, 7d. Low prices, indeed, but a City firm might sell three to four thousand umbrellas a week. Better-class items cost a lot more, of course, an alpaca umbrella being priced at from 6s to 12s, and a good silk umbrella at 22s.

Mass-produced models were dispatched to various shops, such as that of Savoker & Co in Rathbone Place, London, who, besides being drapers and haberdashers, ran a parasol warehouse, which must have enjoyed a somewhat seasonal turnover. To ensure a balanced business throughout the year, other shops maintained a parasol display in their fur department.

Smaller firms provided their own outlets, sometimes selling their products in the same building, the same room even, in which they were made. A few, from modest beginnings, went from strength to strength. Sangster's had been founded in 1777 at 94 Fleet Street, and soon became recognised as leading umbrella-makers. They had a shop in Regent Street in 1839, and established other branches in Cheapside and Cornhill, being perhaps the first umbrella manufacturers to own a chain of shops. Two of the Sangster family, William and John, became famous for their alpaca-covered umbrellas, which had won a prize medal for their excellent quality at the Great Exhibition. Alpaca was inferior to silk, but cheaper at 2s a yard, being made from the undyed wool of South American sheep, and was impervious to sunshine and water. It was destined to become very popular, the English industry using £25,000 worth in 1851, and

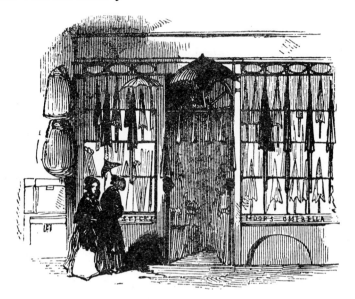

Victorian umbrella shop

selling 45,000 models covered with it in 1854. By 1860, Sangster's are reputed to have been marketing half a million alpaca umbrellas annually.[7]

Well-known by that date was the solid workmanship of several superior firms, whose production methods and equipment changed but little over the years, though their methods of assembly testified to their expert knowledge. They offered a wide range of woods, malacca or whangee being favourites for the handle, which could be fitted and glued to shafts of ash, cherry or lancewood, or whatever else the customer preferred. The frame-maker would use the more efficient notch instead of the primitive system of threading ribs on to a wire (as was still done by many makers), and all stages of production were entrusted to craftsmen and women more highly skilled than was usual. They produced top-class goods, but such work could almost destroy a business, for umbrellas thus manufactured seldom had to be repaired or re-covered. As one might expect, this standard of workmanship has now all but died out, though it could still apply to the occasional firm, such as Brigg's of

Piccadilly, where in the old days perfectionists would call in to have their umbrellas ironed and re-rolled after a shower. 'Ambling down to Brigg's in the morning' proved a popular way to spend a half-hour, during which one could perhaps select a new type of handle to add to one's wardrobe of brollies, Brigg's had by then established a reputation for meeting special orders, providing handles and sticks in one piece, or even accommodating 'one customer, still spoken of with affection and admiration [who] demanded an umbrella with nine ribs instead of the normal eight. He was a member of the Eccentrics Club, but whether *post hoc* or *propter hoc* is not entirely apparent'.[8]

Such superior firms would have sold their own products, or marketed them only through accredited wholesalers, whereas many of the cheaper gamps from the East End were sold in the streets. Henry Mayhew, commenting on this busy trade in his book, *London Labour and the London Poor*, wrote:

> The street-traders in old umbrellas and parasols are numerous, but the buying is but one part, and the least skilled part, of the business. Men, some tolerably well-dressed, some swarthy-looking, like gypsies, and some with a vagabond aspect, may be seen in all quarters of the town and suburbs, carrying a few ragged-looking umbrellas, or the sticks or ribs of umbrellas, under their arms, and crying 'Umbrellas to mend,' or 'Any old umbrellas to sell?' The traffickers in umbrellas are also the crockmen, who are always glad to obtain them in barter, and who merely dispose of them at the Old Clothes Exchange, or in Petticoat lane. . . .
>
> Not so very many years back the use of an umbrella by a man was regarded as partaking of effeminacy, but now they are sold in thousands in the streets, and in the second-hand shops of Monmouth-street and such places. One of these street-traders told me that he had lately sold, but not to an extent which might encourage him to proceed, old silk umbrellas in the streets for gentlemen to protect themselves from the rays of the sun.[9]

Other well-known figures in the trade were the repairers, known in Victorian street-slang as 'mush-fakers', or mushroom-fakers, mushroom being a reference to the form of an expanded umbrella. They, Mayhew reported

> . . . will repair any umbrella on the owner's premises, and their work is often done adroitly, I am informed, and as often bunglingly, or, in the trade term, 'botched'. So far there is no traffic in the business, the

Umbrella seller

mushroom-faker simply performing a piece of handicraft, and being paid for the job. But there is another class of street-folk who buy the old umbrellas in Petticoat lane, or of the street buyer or collector, and 'sometimes', as one of these men said to me, 'we are our own buyers on a round'. They mend the umbrellas—some of their wives, I am assured, being adepts as well as themselves—and offer them for sale on the approaches to bridges, and at the corners of streets.[10]

There were, of course, also shops, usually identifiable by the sign of a red umbrella, which undertook repairs, and no doubt provided a more reliable and comprehensive service than the street men. Such a business, in Old Street, Shoreditch, displayed two curious cards in its window in mid-century. One compared the ailments of umbrellas and humans, whilst the other gave the

Umbrella mender *c* 1833

following prices for repairs at this self-styled Umbrella Hospital.[11]

	s	d
Restoring a broken rib		6
Restoring a spine		6
Inserting a new spine	1	0
Resuscitating the muscularia		6
A new membraneous attachment	2	6
Restoring a shattered constitution	1	0
Setting a dislocated neck		6
Restoring a broken neck		9
A new set of nerves	1	0
A new rib		6
A new muscle		3
A new motive power		6
A crenated attachment		6
Restoring the muscular power	1	6
Fixing on a new head		3
Supplying a new head	1	0

Another service was provided by such firms as the London Umbrella Company which, in mid-century, had posts all over central London from which umbrellas might be hired for a deposit and small fee. Borrowers were given a ticket with the following legend:

> 4sh deposit and 4d for 3 hours or less, up to 9d for from 12–24 hours.
> Each subsequent day 6d.
> Cheaper rate for nights between 9 at night till 9 next morning.
> Deposit back when umbrella returned, with this ticket, at same or any
> station.

    *   *   *   *

The middle years of the century saw various changes as the trade exploited the benefits of the industrial revolution. Japanned iron sticks, tinned iron stretchers and most brass parts (all once near-universal) were relegated to the export trade. Steam was used to produce various parts of umbrella-furniture, and it became possible to make ribs in one operation instead of several.[12] But as late as 1886 the rivetting together of rib and stretcher had not yet 'proved good and economical'. However, there was one further improvement to ribs that was extremely successful and contributed to the brolly's modern shape. In 1873 Fox's announced their patented curved ribs, which made the umbrella look far neater when furled, for the tips now lay closer to the handle instead of encircling it half an inch away and consequently catching in clothing and curtains. These improvements in production methods and the economies in materials enabled manufacturers gradually to reduce prices, sometimes down to half those of the first home-produced umbrellas. (The same mechanical improvements also reduced wages and opportunities for the outworker: 'good money could be made at it while the work lasted, but the idle set is hard on us women.'[13])

Despite all this, overseas competition in the early 'eighties damaged the home trade, for Germany began to export umbrellas to Britain at a price that could not be competed against, the goods often being surplus stock disposed of at cost. British firms had to petition the government to encourage sales and themselves concentrated on exports, so that the values of outgoing products gradually rose, reaching a £665,000 peak in 1888. Export models were generally of poor standard, many of them being made from out-of-date materials by women in the East End of London. A large number went to Asia; in 1882, for instance, 819,313 were sold to Burma, and 3,530,055 to India, as part of that year's £485,137 of exports.

But the German incident was only the prelude to the home industry's steady decline as the result of international rivalry. Very soon even well-established concerns were unable to maintain their independence, and it was not uncommon for a local firm to join with, say, its supplier of steel wire, and then for the hybrid to link up with two or more other firms. The well-known businesses started by Cox and Holland formed part of one five-firm combine. The shrinking number of makers is clearly shown in the successive county directories of the period, but the mergers were not seen to be particularly ominous at the time, being euphemistically described as a major part of the consolidation against overseas competition.[14]

In 1904–6 the trade made another strong bid to increase sales to overseas lands which were not British possessions—so that by 1907 42 per cent of the £1,314,000 national production figures came from exports. But from then on the yearly figures began to dwindle, due to increasing rivalry from Japan and Italy, and it is unlikely that the trade would have recovered its old supremacy even if the next decade had been peaceful. Exports to India, once so important to the British manufacturers, also fell off, but that country still remained the home traders' mainstay, for they sent out £193,000 worth of umbrellas in 1905, more than half the total export figure for the year. But this was exceptional, for India's yearly imports from all countries over this period averaged £164,000.[15]

Inevitably, the outbreak of war in 1914 completely disrupted the balance of trade, the Continental countries faring the worst. France was particularly badly hit, for out of the 1,066,000 umbrellas she had been exporting in 1913, 18 per cent had been going to countries with which she was now at war. Surprisingly, however, her traders continued to receive numerous orders for the duration, including some from China for frames, though they were severely hampered by the acute shortage of labour and materials. More women had to be taught the trade, and the manufacturers had to obtain metal fittings from America and Italy, fabric from England, cane ribs and lacquered handles from Japan, and cane handles from Canton. Orders from the French colonies, Cyprus and Spain had to be refused, with the result that these customers turned to England and Japan.

After the war, the French trade was slow to recover and by the end of 1919 output was only half of the pre-war figure, while the fall in the exchange was prohibiting fabric and metal being purchased from England; exports were a paltry 130,000 umbrellas, 12 per cent of the pre-war figure.[16]

British trade suffered similarly during the war, especially from the enforced limits on production, though it could still rely on the colonies to provide materials, and was able to supply less fortunate countries with fabric. In 1913, exports had totalled 3,518,184 umbrellas valued at £483,452; by 1919 this had fallen to 570,228 at £265,779 (an increase of 235 per cent in the average price of each umbrella sent overseas). The value of umbrellas sold to foreign markets trebled the next year to £762,949, but the actual number only doubled, such was the rise in costs; an umbrella that had cost 14s in 1918 was selling in

M

May 1920 at 35s. Prices began to fall over the next few years, but not before a welcome, if temporary, reprieve had been given to the repairers, whose businesses boomed as more and more people chose to have umbrellas mended rather than replaced. Five times the value of repair work was carried out in 1924, as compared with 1907.

The war brought about other changes in the trade as well, for it speeded up the disappearance of the conscientious craftsman. Employees were now more concerned about their working conditions, and in February 1920 succeeded in establishing a new minimum rate of hourly pay, together with the guarantee of one week's holiday with pay after a year's service. An expert cutter or frame-maker could now earn between 3¾d and 1s 4d an hour, and the less skilled women machinists and fitters up to 9d. Such wages were still far from generous, being about the same as in 1893, when the cost of living was appreciably lower. But that they soon became the minimum is evident from figures for the 1,200 men and 600 women working in the London trade the following year. A boy apprentice could then earn 17s a week, a girl 16s. After their short period of training they would go on to piece-work, with men earning £3 a week, women half that amount. But the industry remained far from attractive to the post-war generation, and with the reduced demand for umbrellas it is not surprising that there was a marked decrease in workshop employees, from 7,563 in 1907 to 5,528 in 1924. There was also a significant change in types of machinery over this period, with internal combustion and water-powered engines being replaced by reciprocating steam engines.[17]

In the next decade, 1925–35, the British trade slumped badly, losing once and for all its grip on the export market in the face of aggressive foreign competition. Some of the new rivals did not necessarily export, but were content to supply their own needs—Hungary was a notable example, cutting her imports to 5 per cent in twelve years. Britain herself sent 1,032,000 umbrellas worth £246,000 abroad in 1924; by 1937, only 432,000 umbrellas at £70,000 were leaving the country.

Worse was to follow when fashion finally dropped the parasol in the early 1930s, and the trade lost this useful summertime

balance to its wet-season counterpart. Nor was it only the production figures that suffered (falling by 18 per cent between 1924
and 1935) but also the public image of the manufacturers, no
longer identified with the gay and light parasol, only with the
dull and utilitarian umbrella.

As Alison Adburgham has put it:

> The shape of an umbrella and a parasol may be identical, the material
> they are made of similar, their handles not unlike; yet there is an
> entirely different atmosphere about them. The umbrella is tainted with
> utility; the parasol is a gay and decorative adjunct. Umbrellas are
> associated with rain and disappointments; parasols, like sundials,
> mark only the summer hours.[18]

Throughout the 'thirties, the home umbrella-manufacturing
trade was faced with ever-increasing competition from abroad,
including the importation of cheap foreign components, and
several steps were taken to protect the home market. Foreign
parts had to be marked with the country of origin, and at least
one firm was fined for failing to observe this requirement.
Purchasers of one of its models could have been under the impression that they were buying a British article—as a buyer for
one retailer had been—when in fact it was foreign. But a director
claimed that it was correct to call the umbrellas British as though
the cloth was Italian, the handles Japanese and the frames
French, the umbrellas had been assembled in London.

Imports of these cheap foreign parts continued, despite the
refusal, in June 1934, of the Import Duties Advisory Com-
mittee to recommend any of the applications for drawback (the
amount of excise or import duty repaid on exports) in the case
of frames. As a result, the rib-makers in particular found that
rising costs were making their wide range of rib sizes uncom-
petitive. Fox's had used 'any and every type of rib' from 16 to
36 inches, but now reduced their stock-range to cover from 18 to
26 inches. In a belated attempt to aid home products, the
Treasury issued an Additional Import Duties Order in March
1937, imposing a duty rate of 20 per cent on most imported
umbrella fittings, and this did encourage the use of British
components for a while.

But at least the British industry was not faring as badly as its counterpart in Germany where the militarisation of its people had put 150,000 umbrella-trade employees out of work. Not for the Nazi the military umbrella, though, as *The Times* suggested, Hitler could have remedied the matter:

> If a Certain Person should, just once, appear in public carrying an umbrella—Or if it should be generally accepted that a certain salute would be all the more impressive if it were made, not with the right arm alone, but with the right arm elongated and ennobled by an umbrella—The spectacle of a hundred thousand umbrellas leaping from their—

Here the writer had to turn from 'fancies so moving as to take away the power of ending a sentence'.[19]

When, five years later, war did come again, most umbrella factories were needed for more important production, though in Britain, at least, a limited output was permitted, a tax having been imposed on all umbrellas in 1940. Raw materials were soon in short supply, and as government departments made allocations to industries rather than to individual firms, the National Federation of Umbrella Manufacturers came into being in 1941 to represent the interests of the industry. On 1 August 1942, the manufacture and repair of umbrellas were forbidden save under licence, and these restrictions remained in force until January, 1947.

Production figures reached their nadir in 1944 when only 540,000 umbrellas left the factories, all destined for the home civilian market. By this time, the acute labour shortage had caused the government to operate a concentration of industry policy, which obliged firms to team up together, with perhaps one factory producing umbrellas for three or four concerns. Many of these firms did not restart as separate entities after the war; in Stepney only two resumed, with ten workers, whereas before the war there had been three firms employing eighty people.[20]

One well-known firm of manufacturers, Sol Schaverien, was turned over to making parts for Mosquito aircraft and for the duration of the war could only produce umbrellas on a small quota basis. Similarly, Samuel Fox became fully engaged in war work, their umbrella department producing stainless steel rims for shrapnel helmets. After Dunkirk, the department switched to turning out gun-belt links for ·303 guns, and later to other forms of vital war material to keep an 'air umbrella' over England. In November 1944, the firm was permitted to resume production of umbrella ribs, and four years later published a centenary book telling its story.[21] When full-scale production was finally resumed, *The Times* commented that:

> . . . it did not, at the time, occur to us that one of the freedoms for which we were fighting was freedom to make umbrellas without permission. . . . Prayers for rain, which, it is understood, constitute the staple devotions of the umbrella-making community, will have been interrupted by a brief service of thanksgiving.[22]

Considering the major break it had suffered in production, the trade made a reasonable post-war comeback in terms of output, though the value figures for 1948 (see table below) are swelled by an increased purchase tax, then at $66\frac{2}{3}$ per cent. Nevertheless the industry went through a difficult period in the post-war years, and in January 1949 a trade deputation called on Douglas Jay, Economic Secretary to the Treasury, to protest against the crippling tax. Mr Jay made the usual promise to bear their representations in mind at the next Budget and, again as usual, no reduction was in fact made, despite overheads having risen 525 per cent since 1938 and prices only 300 per cent. The

COMPARISON OF PRODUCTION FIGURES FOR 1937 & 1938[23]
(Figures for Northern Ireland are very small)

	1937 with N. Ireland	*1948* less N. Ireland
Gross output of establishments with 10+ employees, producing umbrellas & walking-sticks; spare parts included	£1,143,000	£2,225,000
Number of such establishments	about 70	52
Total number of employees	2,854	2,925
Umbrellas sold by such firms	3,780,000	1,512,000
Their value	£823,000	£1,233,000
Umbrellas exported by all firms	432,000	480,000
Their value	£70,000	£355,000

year as a whole proved a very bad one for the trade, with the gross output of the larger firms falling off by £500,000, though this was more than compensated for in 1950. By the end of 1951, sales for the year had topped the two-million mark, and exports of 684,000 models were up on the pre-war figures, though still only a miserable fraction of the trade's export achievements in the late nineteenth century.

Soon, however, Parliament was discussing the imposition of 100 per cent purchase tax on most parts and fittings of umbrellas, to deal with a situation which had arisen out of a firm buying up a number of its moribund competitors with outputs of under £500, and therefore not required to be registered for tax purposes. More than twenty-six of these little companies were purchasing small quantities of parts and arranging for the mother company to make up and market the umbrellas, thus evading purchase tax to the extent of between £10,000 and £20,000 and undercutting other makers by some 8s per model.

The Commons showed little interest in the subject, and though Sir John Barlow, who was also President of the Federation of British Umbrella Manufacturers, urged that a reduction in the purchase tax on complete umbrellas to 33⅓ per cent would remove the temptation to avoid the higher levy, a new Order imposing purchase tax on all parts of an umbrella was approved— and promply drove a number of small firms out of business. Purchase tax on complete models was reduced to 25 per cent in 1953, and that on parts was abolished in 1954, but the trade still complained that the umbrella was really an article of clothing and so merited only 5 per cent purchase tax, instead of being placed in the higher class with walking-sticks.

The years 1954–5 were marked by an alarming increase in the number of umbrellas imported from Hong Kong. Stamped 'Empire Made', these were being imported into Britain at 3s each and sold for 5s 6d. Whole families were making these umbrellas on a cottage-industry basis, working a sixty-hour week on producing frames in their own living quarters. It was estimated the colony could produce 600,000 a month—double the British output. A Manchester tradesman, Walter Mapin, staged a one-man protest march in February 1955, claiming that 5s umbrellas were ruining his business, and that he paid that amount in tax on each of the fifty or sixty models he sold each week. Other dealers pounced on any firm selling umbrellas from Hong Kong that were not stamped with the obligatory 'Empire Made' label.

The first batches of these imports from Hong Kong, being poorly produced and difficult to repair, were badly received by the public, but standards quickly improved, and 'Empire Made' umbrellas were soon cutting deeply into British manufacturers' trade in Africa and the Far East, where half their exports had gone before the war. An even more serious threat was that from Japan, which had smashed the American industry in 1966 by exporting 12,000,000 models to the States within twelve months. 'The history of the Japanese taking over the American umbrella trade has been sobering to us all' commented a home manufacturer with a wary eye to Japanese imports to Britain, which had numbered 318,000 the previous year. This figure nearly doubled the next year, 1966, but fell off to 432,000 in 1967 only because the Japanese concentrated on the German market, where they closed up two-thirds of the industry. Many of the 1,896,000 umbrellas imported into Britain that same year and attributed to Hong Kong were believed to have originated in Japan. All in all, this oriental competition virtually knocked the bottom out of the export market as far as Britain was concerned, for only 26,004 models valued at £39,858 left this country in 1966.

British manufacturers tried to combat the threat by constantly changing colours and designs, knowing that it took overseas firms several months to pick up new trends and market the goods. Efforts were also made to stress the fashionable importance of umbrellas, rather than to rely on their purely utilitarian appeal. Knowing, too, the general attitude of British customers, home traders consoled themselves with the belief that quality and service would tell in the long run. As one British manufacturer put it:

> The American is prepared to buy something and throw it away. The Britisher is not. He expects value for money. If he feels that an article he has bought is not giving him the service he expected, he goes back to the shop from which he bought it. Any reputable manufacturer is prepared to give an after-sales service for his product. He is not

prepared to spend money giving this service to cheap imported
Japanese umbrellas, with the result that people buying these articles
find themselves in trouble when they require mending.[24]

Umbrella-repairing in any event was becoming more and more
a lost art and retailers, finding it impossible to replace their
ageing craftsmen, were obliged to close down their repair departments. Manufacturers were reluctant to undertake the work, as
it interfered with their production of new models, but in 1967
W. Jones & Co introduced a new method of assembly and
marketed their 'Jonesella Jumpex' model, which could be dismantled into three component parts, each of which could easily
be replaced by a retailer.

*   *   *   *

This concluding account of the British umbrella industry's
struggle to survive is not the happiest note on which to end but
even though in Europe, at least, its heyday may have long
passed, the umbrella still retains a wide measure of popularity
and is likely to be with us, in one form or another, for a long
time to come. Young people are not averse to it, and, neatly
rolled, it is still the symbol of the well-dressed businessman;
anglers and golfers are equally addicted to it, and course book-
makers could not function on rainy days without it. Perhaps,
however, the greatest hope for the brolly's future lies in city
centres, as these become increasingly inaccessible to the motorist
through lack of parking space and because of the development of
pedestrian precincts closed to traffic. With the consequent
obligation to walk may come a renewed demand for the umbrella.

The parasol, in its simplest form, is unlikely to stage a comeback, but several firms are happily producing its successors,
giant sun- and advertising umbrellas, colourful and eye-catching,
but yet to acquire the mystique of the ordinary umbrella.

It may even be a portent of what is to come that umbrella-
manufacturers, Sol Schaverien, are now making 'solar radiation
protectors' to shade the pilots of vertical take-off aircraft as they
await final instructions in the cockpit prior to a flight—an
appropriate point, perhaps, at which to leave the umbrella to
find its place in the space-age.

Acknowledgments

S o MANY PEOPLE have kindly given me assistance in obtaining information for this book, that space allows mention here of only a few. Particularly, I would like to thank:
Members of the staff of:
    Devon County Library—Headquarters, and Sidmouth branch
    Exeter City Library
    Exeter University Library
    Church House Library, Sidmouth
    Tunbridge Wells Public Library
    National Reference Library of Science and Invention
    The British Museum
Canon G. S. Foulerton, Cartmel Priory
Barbara Wilder, of S. & W. Griffiths Ltd, Norwich
G. M. Schaefer, Managing Director of Lawtex Ltd, Manchester
Frank Fish, of W. Jones & Co (Umbrellas) Ltd, Sutton, Surrey
James R. Mace Ltd, London
Samuel Fox & Co Ltd, Stocksbridge
B. Ockenden, Secretary to the Federation of British Umbrella Industries
The Oxford University Press, for permission to quote from *Notes & Queries*
Times Newspapers Ltd, for permission to quote from *The Times*

Sources of Information

THIS BOOK IS compiled from an accumulation of facts from some 500 sources consulted by the author, some of which are given below. Much of the information came from books and articles in which sources were not given, thus making it often impossible to check back. (It is one thing to learn that Captain Cook saw native parasols in the South Seas and another to find out where and when; or, knowing of a reference by Honoré de Balzac to the umbrella, to discover the context in which it appeared.) Reference figures in the chapters relate to sources—books, newspapers, correspondence etc—quoted from or extensively used, whilst immediately below are listed works which provided the basic material for several of the chapters.

Boehn, Max von. *Modes and Manners*, Vol 5, 'Ornaments'. (Dent, 1929)

Gordon Cumming, C. F. 'Pagodas, Aurioles and Umbrellas', *The English Illustrated Magazine*, 1887–8, pp 601–12, pp 654–67

Uzanne, Octave. *The Sunshade, the Glove, and the Muff.* (Nimmo & Bain, 1883)

Varron, A. 'The Umbrella', *Ciba Review*, No 42, 1942, pp 1509–48

Scrapbook of newspaper cuttings in the possession of the Federation of British Umbrella Industries

Scrapbook compiled by A. R. Wright, 1910–30, in the possession of the National Reference Library of Science and Invention

Various numbers of *The Times, Notes & Queries, Parapluies et Ombrelles de France,* and *L'Ombrelle e la Moda*

FOREWORD

1 David Piper, 'Geo-brolliology, or Climate and the Umbrella', *The Geographical Magazine*, vol 25, no 8, 1952, p 390
2 *Notes & Queries*, 1st Series, vol 12, p 137
3 Uzanne, op cit, pp 8–9
4 Charles de Linas, 'Les Disques Crucifères, le Flabellum et l'Umbella', *Revue de l'Art Chrétienne*, 1884, pp 5–33
5 cited by Uzanne, op cit, p 62
6 ibid, pp 67–8
7 G. Morrazzoni & C. E. Restelli, *L'Ombrello, contributo alla storia della moda e del costume*, (Milan, 1956)

CHAPTER I
(Titles of classical works are given in their best-known form)

1 Edward Westermarck, *The History of Human Marriage*, (Macmillan, 1921), vol 2, p 529, gives various examples
2 A. T. Olmstead, *History of Palestine and Syria*, (New York, 1931), ch 19, p 291
3 G. Rawlinson, *The Five Great Monarchies of the Ancient Eastern World*, (John Murray, 1879), vol 1, ch 7, pp 495–6
4 ibid, vol 3, ch 3, p 210
5 Herodotus, *Historiae*, bk 2, passage 171
6 Aristophanes, *Thesmophoriazusae*, line 830
7 Aristophanes, *Aves*, lines 1550–1
8 Aristophanes, *Thesmophoriazusae*, lines 821–3
9 Anacreon, *Ap Athenaus*, fragment 66, ch 44
10 Xenophon, *Cyropoedia*, bk 8, ch VIII, passage 17
11 Aristophanes, *Equitibus*, lines 1347–8
12 Ovid, *Fasti*, bk 2, line 311
13 Martial, *Epigrams*, bk 14, no 28
14 ibid, bk 14, no 30
15 Ovid, *Ars Amatoria*, bk 2, line 209
16 Martial, op cit, bk 11, no 73, line 6
17 Juvenal, *Satires*, no 9, lines 50–4
18 Paulus Paciaudus, *De Umbellae Gestatione*, (Rome, 1752), ch 3
19 *Exodus*, ch 26, verses 31 & 33
20 Herodian, *Historia*, bk 5, ch 3
21 Claudian, *The Fourth Consulship of Honorius*, line 340
22 Claudian, *Against Eutropius*, lines 464–5
23 Joseph Needham, *Science and Civilization in China*, (Cambridge University Press, 1965), vol 4, part 2, pp 70–1, 594 et seq

CHAPTER 2

1 Anon, *Two Dissertations, on the Athenian Skirophoria, and on the Mystical Meaning of the Bough and Umbrella in the Skiran Rites*, (London, 1801), ch 3. (This work discusses in a rambling manner the ancient umbrella.)
2 *The Mahabarata, sclokas* 4941–3
3 A. H. Longhurst, *The Story of the Stupa*, (Ceylon Government Press, 1936), ch 2, p 20
4 Dietrich Seckel, *The Art of Buddhism*, (Methuen, 1964), part 2, ch 2, p 128
5 Samuel Purchas, *Purchas his Pilgrims*, (James MacLehose, 1905), vol 3, p 33
6 Charles Ray, 'The Story of the Umbrella', *Pearson's Magazine*, vol 6, 1898, p 40
7 op cit, (London, 1905), p 278
8 Simon de la Loubère, *A New Historical Relation of the Kingdom of Siam*, (London, 1693), p 47
9 Richard Hakluyt, *The Principal Voyages, Traffiques and Discoveries of the English Nation*, (Dent, 1927), vol 3, pp 305–6
10 A. H. & R. Verrill, *America's Ancient Civilizations*, (New York, 1953), ch 3, p 18
11 J. D. Vaughan, *Manners and Customs of the Chinese in the Straits Settlements*, (Singapore, 1879), p 14
12 A. W. Murray and S. Macfarlane, *Journal of a Missionary Voyage to New Guinea*, (London, 1872), p 33
13 Ray, op cit, p 39
14 Sir Henry Yule, editor, *Travels of Marco Polo*, (London, 1875), p 342
15 Sir E. A. Wallis Budge, *The Monks of Kublai Khan, Emperor of China*, (London, 1928), pp 76 & 155
16 Bernard de Montfaucon, *Antiquity Explained and Represented in Sculpture*, (London, 1723), Supplement to vol 5, p 571
17 J. E. Kidder, *Early Japanese Art*, (Thames & Hudson, 1964), pp 86–8, 182
18 Will. H. Edmunds, *Pointers and Clues to the Subjects of Chinese and Japanese Art*, (Sampson Low, 1934), gives further examples of the umbrella in oriental paintings

CHAPTER 3

1 *Travels of Ali Bey*, (London, 1816), vol 1, p 109
2 op cit, (Routledge & Kegan Paul, 1966), ch 4, p 52
3 Thomas Astley, publisher, *A New General Collection of Voyages and Travels*, (London, 1745–6), vol 3, p 43

4   J. A. Skertchley, *Dahomey As It Is*, (London, 1874), p 259
5   Sir Richard Burton, *A Mission to Gelele, King of Dahome*,
    (Routledge & Kegan Paul, 1966), ch 6, p 131 (footnote)
6   ibid, ch, 7, p 152
7   ibid, ch 12, p 209
8   ibid, ch 9, p 187
9   E. L. R. Meyerowitz, *The Divine Kingship in Ghana and Ancient
    Egypt*, (Faber, 1960), p 81
10 E. L. R. Meyerowitz, *The Akan of Ghana*, (Faber, 1958) pp
    120–1
11 T. E. Bowdich, *Mission from Cape Coast Castle to Ashantee*,
    (London, 1873), ch 2, p 37
12 ibid, ch 3, p 64
13 Kofi Antuban, *Ghana's Heritage of Culture*, (Leipzig, 1963),
    pp 150–1
14 *Illustrated London News*, 21 March 1874, p 278
15 A. A. Kiperemateng, *Panoply of Ghana*, (Longmans, 1964), pp
    89–91
16 Sir S. W. Barker, *The Nile Tribes of Abyssinia*, (Macmillan,
    1908), ch 21, p 366
17 op cit, (Methuen, 1897), ch 7, p 187, appendix 2, 'Hints on Out-
    fit'
18 *Notes & Queries*, 4th series, vol 8, p 338
19 Commander V. L. Cameron, *Across Africa*, (London, 1877),
    vol 1, ch 12, p 207
20 R. A. Freeman, *Travels and Life in Ashanti and Jaman*, (Frank
    Cass, 1967), ch 2, p 56

CHAPTER 4

1   Caedmon, *Genesis*, line 813
2   Phillipe des Reimes, *Blonde of Oxford and Jehan of Dammartin*,
    (Camden Society, 1858), lines 2675–82
3   Mgr Horace Mann, *Lives of the Popes in the Middle Ages*, (Lon-
    don, 1902), vol 1, part 2, p 467
4   Zsolt Aradi, *The Popes*, (Macmillan, 1956), ch 2, pp 59–60
5   Gordon Cumming, op cit, p 661
6   Louisa Twining, *Christian Symbols and Emblems*, (John Murray,
    1885), p 203
7   The copy is now in the British Museum (Harleian Manuscripts,
    no 603)
8   Linas, op cit, pp 22–4
9   ibid, p 25
10 ibid, p 26
11 loc cit

CHAPTER 5

1   Quoted by Therle Hughes, *Small Antiques for the Collector*,
    (Lutterworth, 1964), ch 7, p 82. This is the earliest record of an
    actual umbrella in Britain, and probably comes from the queen's
    wardrobe book. Mrs Hughes appears to be the only writer to
    have noted this model.
2   Uzanne, op cit, p 29. Other Continental allusions in this chapter
    are usually taken from Uzanne's book.
3   ibid, p 30
4   Michel de Montaigne, *Essais de la Vanité*, bk 3, ch 9
5   Roy C. Strong, 'Sir Henry Unton and his Portrait—an Eliza-
    bethan Memorial Picture and its History', *Archaeologia*, vol 99,
    pp 53–76
6   Robert Parke, translator, *Gonzalez de Mendoza's History of the
    Great and Mighty Kingdom of China*, (Hakluyt Society, 1853),
    vol 2, p 105
7   Hakluyt, op cit, vol 3, p 299
8   Sir Edmund Gosse, editor, *The Life and Letters of John Donne*,
    (Massachusetts, 1959), the letter to Sir Henry Goodyer, Vol 1, p 220
9   Purchas, op cit, vol 19, p 19
10 Ben Jonson, *The Devil is an Ass*, act 4, scene 1
11 Tom Coryate, *Crudities*, (London, 1611), vol 1, p 134
12 E. M. Thompson, editor, *The Diary of Richard Cocks*, (Hakluyt
    Society, 1883), vol 1, p 28
13 Fynes Moryson, *An Itinerary*, (James MacLehose, 1908), vol 3,
    p 391
14 op cit, act 3, scene 1, lines 1–4
15 Michael Drayton, *The Muses Elizium*—the Second Nimphall,
    lines 167–74
16 Moryson, op cit, vol 4, p 215
17 op cit, act 2, scene 1
18 John Lough, editor, *Locke's Travels in France, 1675–79*, (Cam-
    bridge University Press, 1953), p 41
19 op cit, no 1721/4, 16 May 1682
20 op cit, no 16, 19 February 1718, p 109
21 op cit (Dent's Everyman's Library, 1964), p 121
22 op cit, act 3, scene 1
23 op cit, lines 31–8
24 John Gay, *Trivia*, bk 1, lines 209–18
25 ibid, bk 2, lines 57–60
26 William Hone, *The Every-Day Book and Table Book*, (London,
    1839), vol 4, column 101; see also William Andrews, editor and
    publisher, *Old Church Life* (1900), pp 224–30
27 *Notes & Queries*, 5th series, vol 7, p 158

CHAPTER 6

1   quoted in *Notes & Queries*, 1st series, vol 1, p 414
2   Jonas Hanway, *Travels thro Russia into Persia*, (London, 1753), vol 2, ch 42, p 286
3   John Pugh, *Remarkable Occurrences in the Life of Jonas Hanway*, (London, 1787)
4   Letter from Mrs. Strong to the secretary of the Marine Society, July 1895; see Captain H. T. A. Bosanquet, 'A Forthcoming Bicentenary—Jonas Hanway and his Umbrella', *The Mariner Magazine*, 15 August 1955, p 48
5   P. J. Grosley, *A Tour to London*, (1772), vol 1, p 45
6   Mrs Paget Toynbee, editor, *The Letters of Horace Walpole*, (Clarendon Press, 1904), vol 6, p 309
7   Sir W. R. Drake, *Heathiana*, (London, 1881), p 21
8   cited by Uzanne, op cit, pp 41–2
9   M. Dorothy George, *Catalogue of Political and Personal Satires in Department of Prints and Drawings, British Museum*, print no 4918
10 John Beresford, editor, *Woodforde*, (Oxford University Press, 1935), p 241
11 A. M. Gummere, *The Quaker*, (Philadelphia, 1901), pp 48–50
12 E. S. Curtis, *The North American Indian*, (Cambridge, Massachusetts, 1908), vol 3, appendix, p 168
13 James Stockdale, *Annales Caremoelenses*, (Ulverston, 1872); this includes various references to early umbrellas, including the one at Cartmel Priory.
14 cited by Uzanne, op cit, p 42
15 *The Report of the Juries* [of the Great Exhibition], (London, 1852), p 658
16 The anecdotes in this paragraph come from early numbers of *Notes & Queries*
17 *Kirby's Wonderful and Scientific Museum*, (London, 1804), vol 2, p 49
18 John MacDonald, *Memoirs of an Eighteenth Century Footman*, (London, 1790), pp 381–3
19 Communicated by Norman Penney, *Notes & Queries*, vol 148, p 133
20 From an unspecified number of the *Glasgow Constitutional*, as quoted in *The Penny Magazine*, 2 January 1836, pp 5–7
21 George, op cit, print nos 5793, 6132, and 6743; the latter print, *A Battle of Umbrellas*, accompanied a satirical essay of the same title, but most irrelevant, in *The Wit's Magazine*, vol 1, 1 September 1784, pp 286–8
22 op cit, bk 4, lines 550–2

23 R. L. Stevenson, with J. W. Ferrier, 'The Philosophy of Um-
    brellas', *Edinburgh University Magazine*, January–April, 1871;
    later reprinted in *The Works of R. L. Stevenson*, vol 22, 'Juvenilia',
    (Chatto & Windus, 1912), p 62
24 Communicated by F. C. H., *Notes & Queries*, 4th series, vol 8,
    p 492
25 George, op cit, print no 8685 (*Copenhagen House*, engraved by
    H. Humphrey)
26 Many of these aeronautical details come from E. Hodgson, *The
    History of Aeronautics in Great Britain*, (Oxford University
    Press, 1924)
27 See *The Mariner's Mirror*, vol 34, pp 219–20 for further details

CHAPTER 7

Those wishing to read more about the fashionable parasol are
referred to the following, all of which were used when compiling this
chapter:

Buck, A. M. *Victorian Costume and Costume Accessories*, (Herbert
    Jenkins, 1961), ch 18, pp 179–83
Davenport, Milla. *The Book of Costume*, (New York, 1948)
Hughes, Therle. 'The Fashion for Parasols', *Country Life*, 5 Decem-
    ber 1963; and
    Small Antiques for the Collector, (Lutterworth), ch 7, pp 82–95
Lester, K. M., & Oerke, B. V. *Accessories of Dress*, (Illinois, 1954),
    part 5, ch 30, pp 402–14
and such Victorian magazines as *The Young Englishwoman, World of
Fashion, Englishwoman's Domestic Magazine*, and *Lady's Companion*

 1 A. M. Cohn, *George Cruikshank—A Catalogue Raisonné*,
    (London, 1924), p 349
 2 George, op cit, print no 15351; the print itself was published in
    The Northern Looking-Glass, new series, vol 1, no 2, May 1826,
    p 5
 3 From a letter to Paris, quoted by E. McClellan, *History of
    American Costume, 1607–1870*, (New York, 1937), p 383
 4 Uzanne, op cit, p 53
 5 Professor Wilson, *Noctes Ambrosianae*, (Edinburgh, 1868), vol 4,
    p 220; this is a collection of essays formerly published in *Black-
    wood's Magazine* between 1822 and 1835
 6 Uzanne, op cit, p 57
 7 *The Art Union*, 1848, vol 10, p 364
 8 *Abridgements of Specifications relating to Umbrellas, Parasols
    and Walking-Sticks*, 1760–1866 (London, 1871); these give
    details of the various brainwaves, with references to the original
    patents

9 Frank Rede Fowke, 'Umbrellas', *The Gentleman's Magazine*, vol 266, 1889, p 543

10 Uzanne, op cit, pp 63–4

11 The Duke of Windsor, *A King's Story*, (Cassell, 1951), ch 16, p 282

12 *The Times*, 27 October 1936, p 15

CHAPTER 8

1 General Cavalié Mercer, *Journal of the Waterloo Campaign*, (Peter Davies, 1927), ch 13, p 165

2 Many of these military anecdotes have been told by R. Hargreaves, 'Brollies and Gold Lace', *Chambers' Journal*, 9th series, vol 1, pp 205–8; see also E. R. Yarham, 'The Umbrella Front: Gamps on the Battlefield', *The Army Quarterly*, November 1942, pp 75–9

3 *St Swithin's Chapel; 'Cold-bath Fields'*, sketched, engraved and published by George Cruikshank, December 1833

4 Various of these later military anecdotes were told in *The Times* between 16 October and 7 November 1934.

5 As quoted by Uzanne, op cit, pp 62–3

6 ibid p 65

7 *The Times*, 1 July 1868, p 11

8 ibid, 20 May 1872, p 7

9 H. F. Jones, *Samuel Butler, a Memoir*, (Macmillan, 1920), vol 1, ch 20, p 370

10 Stevenson, op cit, p 62

11 Sabine Baring-Gould, *Strange Survivals*, (Methuen, 1894), ch 6, pp 130–1

12 See the correspondence columns of *The Times*, 23–8 September 1957

CHAPTER 9

1 Daniel Defoe, *Robinson Crusoe*, in The Works of Daniel Defoe (Edinburgh, 1869), p 74

2 Stevenson, op cit, p 62

3 As cited in source note 1 of ch 2

4 op cit, pp 13–14

5 ibid, pp 29–30

6 ibid, p 28

7 'Umbrellas in the East', *The Penny Magazine*, 5 December 1835, pp 479–80; see also the sequel, 'Umbrellas', in the issue of 2 January 1836, pp 5–7

8 René-Marie Cazal, *Essai Historique, Anecdotique, sur le Parapluie, l'Ombrelle et la Canne*, (Paris, 1844)

N

9 For further details see E. T. Ward, 'Gamps', *The Dickensian*, vol 24, no 205, pp 41–3
10 'The Umbrella', *Household Words*, vol 6, 1853, pp 201–4
11 See especially Isaac D'Israeli, 'Of Domestic Novelties at First Condemned', *The Literary Character*, (London, 1862), pp 358–9
12 Information from the Mitchell Library, Glasgow; the advertisements appear in Joseph Wright, *Laird Nicoll's Kitchen, and other Scottish stories* (18th edition, Glasgow, 1893)
13 George Borrow, *Wild Wales*, (John Murray, 1907), ch 71, p 470 and footnote
14 G. V. Cox, *Recollections of Oxford*, (Macmillan, 1868), p 298
15 William Sangster, *Umbrellas and their History*, (London, 1855), ch 5, p 68
16 Sir Walter Scott, editor, *The Secret History of the Court of James I*, (Edinburgh, 1811), p 188
17 A. G. Gardiner, *Pebbles on the Shore*, (J. M. Dent, 1925), pp 52–6
18 Ivor Brown, 'Put up More Gamps', *The Observer*, 26 April 1953
19 J. G. Wilson, editor, *Life and Letters of Fitz Greene Halleck*, (New York, 1869), p 494
20 Ray, op cit, p 42
21 As cited in source note 1 to ch 5
22 But see Clyde & Black, *Umbrellas and their History*; this is a very obscure book published in New York, in 1864

CHAPTER 10

1 'Senex' (Robert Reid), *Glasgow Past and Present* (1884), vol 2, p 182
2 B. W. Clapp, *John Owens, Manchester Merchant*, (Manchester University Press, 1965), ch 2, pp 18–20; ch 3, pp 22–4
3 Statistics as quoted in *The Report of the Juries*, p 658
4 Stanley Moxon, *Umbrella Frames, 1848–1948*, (Samuel Fox, 1948), tells the full story of Fox and his work
5 op cit, pp 658–9
6 ibid, p 659
7 Alison Adburgham, *Shops and Shopping, 1800–1914*, (Allen & Unwin, 1964), ch 10 has provided some of the information concerning retailers and hiring firms given in this chapter
8 Thomas Girtin, *Makers of Distinction*, (Harvill Press, 1959), ch 5, p 84; this book, pp 80–9, also provided the preceding information on high-class umbrella manufacture
9 op cit, (Frank Cass, 1967), vol 2, p 115
10 loc cit
11 J. Larwood & J. C. Hotten, *The History of Signboards*, (London, 1866), p 413

12 See Samuel Timmins, editor, *Birmingham and the Midland Hardware District*, (Frank Cass, 1967,) pp 667–8, for details of the various developments

13 For further details of the hardship of people in the umbrella trade, see Charles Booth, *Life and Labour of the People in London*, (Macmillan, 1893), vol 4, ch 9, pp 268–70; and E. Cadbury, et al, *Woman's Work and Wages*, (London, 1906), appendix, p 318

14 For contemporary opinion, see 'Midland Captains of Industry', *Birmingham Gazette & Express*, 20 December 1907, pp 83–4

15 *The Bag, Portmanteau and Umbrella Trader*, 1907–21, will provide much detailed information for those wishing to know more about the trade during this period

16 Arthur Fontaine, *French Industry during the War*, (New Haven, 1926), ch 12, pp 224–5 appendix 32, pp 442–3

17 *The Board of Trade Journal*, 21 July 1927, p 6

18 Adburgham, op cit, ch 10, p 112

19 *The Times*, 16 October 1934, p 15

20 Information about the war period was supplied by B. Ockenden, Secretary to the Federation of British Umbrella Industries

21 See above, source note 4; the firms of Sangster's and Kendall's have also been connected with publications about their products; see source note 15 of ch 9; also Harry J. French, *Umbrellas Past and Present*, (Kendall's, 1923).

22 *The Times*, 27 January 1947, p 5

23 The Board of Trade, Final Report on the Census of Production for 1948, vol 7, Trade K, Umbrellas & Walking Sticks (HMSO, 1951)

24 Communication from Frank Fish of W. Jones & Co (Umbrellas) Ltd

Index

Illustrations are indicated by italic figures